BEVERLY HILLS PRINCIPAL

. . . there was a "Happening" at the Flagpole.

A STORY OF LEADERSHIP DURING THE TIME THAT UNRAVELED AMERICA

by
F. Willard Robinson, Ed.D
Beverly Hills High School
Beverly Hills, California

Copyright © 1999 F. Willard Robinson, Ed.D.
All rights reserved. This book, or parts thereof, may not be
reproduced or publicly performed in any form without permission.

Published by
Writers Press, Boise, ID 83706

Printed in the United States of America

Library of Congress Catalog No.
98-87093

I.S.B.N. 1-885101-72-4

to Joan. . .
*Who is such an integral part of this history.
Without her love, support and counsel,
this would surely have been a different story.*

Foreword

Robbie Robinson was my principal. With courage and compassion, accepting the Lord's transforming love, Robbie led Beverly Hills High School through the turbulent years of the sixties and seventies. His emerging leadership style enabled many of the students and faculty to experience a new fullness of grace unencumbered by the force of human will.

The Gospel of Matthew records that Jesus *when he saw the crowds, he had compassion on them because they were harassed and helpless, like sheep without a shepherd*. Whoever one may say Jesus is, he is not some celestial special prosecutor sent to earth to indict us mortals before an angelic grand jury for our multiple shortcomings and sins. Certainly those Roman times were as corrupt as our times. And they were no different from even earlier days when the Psalmist lamented, *Why do the evil prosper?* Yet the Christ did not come to condemn but to love, to forgive and to save. This is the truth that was revealed anew to our principal when he was under fire. In those dramatic days of polarization when on one side there was the call to assert the full authority of the establishment, and on the other side, the call to surrender to immature idealism or anarchy, Robbie found the *unforced rhythms of grace*. Indeed our principal, learned what the Psalmist meant when he recorded, *I sought the Lord and he answered me; he delivered me from my fears*.

Read Beverly Hills Principal joyfully and find renewal, intellectually and spiritually.

The Honorable Eric W. Valentine
Circuit Judge, State of Oregon

Acknowledgements

I give acknowledgement for support and help in the preparation of this manuscript to:

• Bob Freedman who helped capture the essence of Beverly Hills culture as he understood it.

• Lyle Suter, a member of the Beverly Hills High School faculty who suggested the title, *BEVERLY HILLS PRINCIPAL*. "So much of what is written about Beverly Hills is fantasy," he said. "This story is refreshing because it is the *truth*."

• Kenneth L. Peters, retired Superintendent of the Beverly Hills Unified School District whose distinctive leadership qualities gives the story *punch*.

• Don Dutcher of Boise, Idaho for his editing and computer assistance.

• John Ybarra of Writers Press for his enthusiasm, counsel and willingness to be a part of this project.

• Gail Robinson Van Camp, who encouraged me to complete the project and transferred the original text to computer.

"Robbie" Robinson

Preface

From 1959 until 1976, I held the position of Principal at Beverly Hills High School in Beverly Hills, California.

Now, in retrospect, I see how that troublesome time has affected our lives today. A generation has passed. There is merit in recalling the cultural confrontation that has changed our nation and its institutions.

Life, under the relentless passage of time, moves on. How easy it is to forget the lessons we would do well to remember. Some of the dynamics that existed between administrators and students in the high schools and universities of the 1960's can be present between leaders and their people today. This is true in corporate, religious and political institutions as well. For persons who seek new dimensions in the quality of their leadership, and we are all leaders at some level, the experience I relate may provide insight and encouragement.

Rebellious youth of the sixties fought naively to build a New World. But those of us in leadership too often confused force with strength and at times could be inflexible and insensitive in our approach. As a result, leaders often became part of the problem rather than enablers of creative solutions. We all had a lot to learn.

When there is spiritual redemption, leaders in all areas of life can become more sensitive to those with whom they work, moving out in a new strength to accomplish the task before them. You will see an emerging model of *Servant Leadership* in these pages. Today's institutions need nothing less. It is my hope that this story will illustrate this truth.

1

Escape From Death

As principal of Beverly Hills High School in the early 1960s I had gained an envied position of success, being much admired as an efficient and innovative administrator. Then the winds of change swept across campus and I slipped from an apparent life of total self-control to a dismal, disturbing world of self-doubt, growing isolation and shaken confidence. Unprepared, I was being thrust into one of the most turbulent periods of our national history. Caught in the eye of the hurricane, the disruptive events of rebellion swirled across the life of the campus. My style of leadership was being seriously challenged and my position as principal was in immediate danger.

It had been a long road in coming to this crisis. To fully understand my response to the hostile events that could either lead to failure or recovery, I will review the events of life that established my perspective. It is only within the light of awareness that the dark days can gain some illumination.

Let me begin the story with another time of crisis in our nation's history. The perilous times of World War II have become little more than a remote event for some, but the five years I spent as a torpedo pilot in the Navy are as real to me over fifty years later as if they had happened yesterday. The crisis I faced on March 23, 1944 led directly to my commitment as a teacher following the war and my ultimate position as principal of Beverly Hills High School. My escape from death was a miracle.

The long awaited attack on the coral fortress of Kwajalein was under way. The February 1944 issue of Time Magazine describes the engagement:

> *Admiral Nimitz threw into the attack the greatest naval force ever concentrated on a single military objective. The Japanese were not surprised at the sight of the birds sweeping up from the horizon. For twenty-two successive days the birds had come, scattering destruction over the coral fortress. Down came the planes in screaming dives, driving the enemy deeper and deeper into their concrete pillboxes. The atoll shuddered under the impact of bomb upon bursting bomb from the carrier-based planes. The United States forces had moved into the Marshall Islands domain for the kill. The weeks count has been 400 Japanese planes destroyed: U.S. loss only sixty planes.*

Undeniably, there was a tremendous sense of exhilaration to be a part of this dramatic striking force. One day I counted 220 planes around me as I led a torpedo-bombing section into the Japanese-held territory. We were attached to Torpedo Squadron VC-7 operating from the aircraft carrier, Manila Bay. The Grumman Avengers we were flying could engulf a torpedo within the fuselage, a ton of bombs or four 500-pound depth charges. Our squadron was the first in the history of war to fire aerial rockets. We carried them on this mission. It was an important development at the time, for in one salvo, the plane could send a battery of eight exploding warheads into an enemy target. Having this lethal force at my fingertips, and feeling like an important cog in the greatest striking force ever assembled did stir great feelings of unique value within me.

But there was another side, one I dared not verbalize. I was feeling less than heroic. What chance did these little men have under the rain of bombs? They faced an inevitable death, hostage to the system under which by chance they were born. Was this what God had prepared for me? I tried without success to shut down the conflict within me. And then, too, I sensed a deep underlying uneasiness that time was running out. Call it premonition, I don't know. It was with some apprehension that I wrote what possibly would be my last letters home.

That night I found it difficult to sleep. Our quarters were directly over the storage area for the high-test gasoline used in our planes. There was no armor plate on these light little carriers to protect us from the stalking enemy submarines. I had a number of good friends from our training days in Corpus Christi, Texas, who had been wiped out in one blinding flash as the carrier Liscombe Bay went down in fire two months earlier off Tarawa. They never got out of their cabins. We had minimal protection on these escort aircraft carriers. The little freedom I felt was when I was in the sky or at night where sometimes I would sit in the cockpit of my TBF. There I felt the tropical air blowing in the night, and it was a solace. The Japanese submarines were always with us.

Commander Gene Breen, an Annapolis graduate, briefed us in the ship's ready-room. There, just below the flight deck, the pilots gathered to get the strike orders. In this confined area, distinguished by a combined odor of stale tobacco, nervous perspiration and a residue of hydraulic fluid on the flyers soiled flight gear, we were briefed for our missions. On this day of crisis I was assigned to fly an individual scout and patrol in a relative 30-degree vector for 100 miles west-northwest of the fleet.

No sooner had I completed the necessary calculations for the flight on my plotting board than the abrupt order came over the ships sound system, "Pilots man your planes."

I swung up the ladder and onto the busy flight deck where my crew was waiting. A special bond grows among the men who share the strain and uncertainties of long hours together in the air.

"Are you ready, George?"

"Ready, Skipper!"

It was the radioman, George Driesback, Jr., a blond, sharp youth from Rockford, Illinois. His father was proud of George's engagement at Attu, in Alaska. Harold Eckert was already in the turret. He was the gunner, a quiet, purposeful boy from Los Angeles who seldom talked while in the air. Harold was keen, cool and an excellent shot.

Old *Jo-Do*, our regular plane, was anchored down near the fantail and we were scheduled early off in a new plane to the fleet, a Grumman Avenger (TBM-3E) that I had never flown before. I knew I would miss the *old-shoe* feeling of a plane that had grown to be a part of me. But that was the way it was in naval carrier warfare. Dispatch in flying a squadron off is of primary concern. For this reason a navy pilot does not always get his regular plane.

Again, the loudspeaker from the bridge sounded, "Pilots start your engines."

Cautiously, I taxied the bomber into position. The bright-shirted men of the deck crew, laboring in the turbulent air, attached the cable yoke to the undercarriage of the plane while I adjusted the leather headrest, made a final check of the instrument panel and built up the power to check the magnetos. The Wright 2600 rotary engine responded with a steady roar.

While this preparation was under way, the men below deck worked to build up the pressure of oil and compressed air for the catapult shot. The final check had been completed. I pushed the throttle forward to the firewall, and the big bird responded, screeching and trembling within the cable yoke that held us.

"Ready George? Ready Harold?"

"Ready Captain."

I lifted my hand and moved it in a horizontal direction from left to right, the signal for release. Whooosh! The Avenger was catapulted, accelerating to ninety knots as it left the bow of the flight deck.

We were free of the carrier, but the 2000 pounds of torpex depth charges and the full load of rockets and fuel were forcing the laboring plane to the wave tops. Our take-off was alarmingly sluggish.

The navy had the facility for taking a fine airplane and then, with each succeeding modification, hanging on enough extra gear to cut in on its original performance. I was convinced this was what happened to our TBM-3E.

For several nerve-wracking seconds, a laboring propeller was all that stopped us from bellying into the sea. A mile went under us before there was a perceptible change. Then gradually we began to climb. When the moments of tension were shed, we looked down on a task force of ships that literally filled the ocean. I don't know how many, but there were ships in every direction as far as we could see. Five carriers moved at the center of the task force with battleships and cruisers forming the intermediate ring. Interspersed were tankers, military transports, cargo ships and landing craft. Flying our assigned initial heading of 270 degrees, it was not long before we flew beyond the outer circle of destroyers picketing the strike force as a protection against the prowling submarines.

"Quite a sight, don't you think, Skipper?" George was always the more talkative of the crew.

The afternoon passed with routine monotony. At 1600 hours we passed over a Japanese-held atoll, a beautiful spot where the water lightened to the color of a rare turquoise. We saw no enemy activity and flew on.

From periodic radio reports, it became apparent a rescue mission was under way for a TBM which had crashed during the afternoon's operation. I found out later the entire crew had been killed, including Raymond Clapper, the noted war correspondent, "a victim of his own belief that the only way to write a wartime column was to see the war first hand," as the Los Angeles Times later reported. Little did I realize at that moment how close I was to experiencing the mystery into which he had moved.

The setting sun was casting its trail of fire across the water as we headed back toward the task force. Then the silent radio came alive with chatter between airplot and some of the pilots who had made contact with an enemy submarine. I quickly plotted the location on my navigational chart and altered my homeward course with the hope that I could make contact. By the time I arrived I could see where the depth charges had exploded and some oil slicks, but I never was certain about the actual outcome of this contact. I was disappointed that I had not had the opportunity to drop my depth charges. Logistics and economy dictated that I save them for another mission, but there was always an added risk in bringing these heavy loads aboard.

Almost five hours had passed since we had left the Manila Bay and it was a relief to find her in the dusk as night was fast closing down on the fleet.

The landing flight pattern is well defined. We flew up-wind, passed well to the starboard of the fantail and paralleled the course of the ship to a point several hundred yards ahead of the carrier. We began our 180 degree turn to the left, losing altitude, wheels down, flaps down, tail hook down, mixture rich, cowls open, propeller in low pitch and air speed reduced. We eased into the downwind leg of the approach.

I steadied the plane for the final turn that would bring us up the groove and into the directing arms of the landing signal officer. It is a powered approach, the bomber held just above its stalling speed. When the final signal to cut the throttle is given, the plane drops on the deck. Then the tailhook grabs the arresting cable, jerking the heavy plane to an abrupt stop.

When I turned into the downwind leg, I experienced the same problem that had plagued our take-off. Once the speed was reduced to ninety knots, normally the desired setting, there was not enough power, even with the throttle wide open, to hold the loaded plane in the air. It was too late to jettison the explosives! Without warning the plane lurched and trembled. Like a goose hit in the left wing by a volley of shot, we plummeted into the Pacific with terrifying finality. The plane smashed into the water in a death dive, instantly exploding in a shattering burst of water and debris. Before the first plumes of spray slowly fell back, the rolling body of the ocean quivered and exploded four more times as each 500-pound depth charge sent great geysers into the red-streaked sky. Cascades of water turned me over and over. Flashes of light stunned my eyes; green, yellow and purple within an abysmal spectrum. More water engulfed me as I struggled for the surface and air. Like lethal fists, the concussions hit my tumbling body.

With tremendous effort I tripped the release on one side of my Mae West life jacket. It inflated and supported my head. The passing of this storm left me bobbing amidst an unreal quietness. I looked around. All were gone; the flight crew, the plane, even the debris which usually floats from a crash. I was hurt and helpless, but numbness from shock and the realization that I was still alive shielded me from pain.

Soon, a destroyer rolling wings of water from its bow cut toward me. "For God's sake, there's a man alive out there. Full reverse! Full reverse! Get a line over." The orders blasted over the ship's speakers from the bridge. The ship veered and, in an instant a life preserver, attached to the ship by a line, plopped within my reach. Instinctively, almost blindly, I locked my arms around the life preserver and was immediately and violently jerked into a turbulence of water caused by the reverse action of the ship's screws. Desperately I clung to the recovery line.

The destroyer slowed rapidly. Violent whirlpools sucked me down and under the ship. Here was yet another abyss, one that took me to another danger under the slugging blades of the ship's propellers. Would I never come to the surface again? It was an eternity, but with a power that sometimes comes in desperation, I clung to the lifeline. Eventually, the ship stopped dead in the water and I was pulled to the surface. Partially conscious, I again heard the shouting of orders, "Go overboard and secure the line around him. He's still alive!"

A young seaman jumped overboard, wrapped his strong arms around me and the crew on deck lifted us out of the water and hauled us aboard. I was in a state of shock; it seemed somehow unreal.

Sometime during the night I became aware of the ship's cabin where I lay in bed. For the first time, too, I became conscious of pain. An officer entered the dimly lit room, his insignia leaves reflected a dull silver above the points of his khaki collar. His dark hair was specked with gray. His face was lined, almost as if sculpted by the wind and sun from long watches at sea. But his eyes were clear, and I saw in them a loneliness of command and prolonged responsibility.

"You're going to be all right," he said. His voice

was deliberate and reassuring. "I'm going to keep you here in my bunk until we can make contact with a hospital ship. Welcome to our destroyer. I'm Abraham Lincoln, commanding officer, and you are on the U.S.S. Caldwell."

I shall never forget him, not only because he commanded the men who by fate had saved my life, but also because this Abraham Lincoln became a symbol of my day of personal reprieve.

As I lay in bed I began to reconstruct the events of the crash and to determine the extent of my injuries. I remembered I had slipped out of the straps of the parachute and opened the hatch over the cockpit as the plane lowered below 500 feet on our approach to the ship. This was standard procedure.

The engine and left wing hit the water in a nose-dive. I could remember this. The shoulder harness must have held me at the time of impact, but my hand had been on the release lever and the initial explosion must have simultaneously pulled my hand free with the lever and ejected me many yards from the disintegrating plane. It was apparent that I could not have survived without being some distance from the exploding torpex charges, armed by the force of the crash. This is the best explanation I could think of to explain my survival.

My right leg was ripped open and shrapnel was imbedded near the base of my spine. My face was gashed and I suffered *contusions, lacerations and multiple blast injuries.* That's what my medical tag read, when a month later, I was taken in a stretcher off the U.S.S. Relief at Pearl Harbor and transferred to the Base 8 Naval Hospital.

The impact from the explosive force of the depth

charges did a lot of damage to my capillaries and this bleeding under the skin caused extensive distortion and discoloration of my body. The healing process, which took many months, was a difficult time both emotionally and physically. The experience of prolonged pain was new for me and I found it difficult to keep a positive spirit. But, four months later, I was able to take my first steps and healing did gradually come.

As I look back on the miraculous events that led to my survival, two related incidents had significance in my search for a personal God. The evening before our final flight from the Manila Bay, George Driesback, the nineteen-year old radioman, and I were talking on the flight deck.

After a short silence he confessed "I'm afraid. Everything just seems to be building up. I don't know." And there was a thoughtful pause. "Would you pray with me?"

"George," I said cockily, "You do the praying and I'll do the flying." How that cruel response has haunted me. George died that afternoon with the gunner. Could I ever be forgiven or forgive myself?

The second incident occurred long after the sun dropped into the Pacific on that fateful March afternoon. I lay alone on the Captain's bunk. Each partial breath I took was a major physical accomplishment forged in pain. For the first time in over two years, I prayed to God. It was a prayer for George and Harold. I felt responsible for their deaths and was filled with grief, sorrow and despair. I felt guilty that I had been spared, and yet needed to express my thankfulness to God, for through a fate I still do not understand, I was given an undeserved chance for continued life.

During the summer of 1944, I was transferred from Hawaii to the Long Beach Naval Hospital where I had an emotional reunion with the love of my life. Joan and I were together again, and she was a major factor in my continued healing.

Before the war was over I returned for another assignment in the western Pacific which took me into the Solomon Islands, New Guinea, the Admiralty Islands, and then home at last. The war ended. I was ready to return to civilian life. Now, as a patriotic American war veteran and responsible husband, I would grit my teeth, step forward and conquer my world.

2

In The Beginning

Like most families who were involved in the Westward Movement, my ancestors were strong God fearing people. Their very survival depended upon a physical and emotional strength I only began to fully appreciate as I matured. They were people of courage with an inbred sense of right and wrong. Compromise was weakness. Most issues were reduced to right or wrong. One should fight the devil and God would help those who helped themselves. Their word was their bond, their ethic was work and they displayed the stamina of the true pioneer. This was the legacy of our land as well as my personal legacy.

My grandparents on both sides of the family arrived or were born in California in the forty-year period between 1859 and 1890, were married in the state and established the homes in which my parents were born.

My paternal grandfather often told me about his trip in a covered wagon from St. Joseph, Missouri to California. He was four years old, so his memory of Indian encounters and the perilous journey were quite vivid. Led by his father, who had been elected the leader, the train of wagons followed the trail westward along the Platte River, over the continental divide at South Pass, through the Humboldt Sink in Nevada and then across the Sierra above Donner Lake, to

Sacramento. My Grandfather Robinson became a Methodist minister, an evangelist and an early circuit rider preaching in frontier communities throughout the state. He had been a successful farmer in the San Joaquin Valley until he received a *direct call from God* to preach. This he did, at a great economic and emotional sacrifice to his own family.

My maternal grandfather arrived in California with his parents and established a family homestead in southern Monterey County near the little frontier settlement of Parkfield. His wife, my grandmother, had been raised in a Southern family of culture. She came west to marry a stagecoach driver!

When my great-grandfather fenced in his homestead, his action was met with hostility from the cattlemen who had controlled the open range without challenge. One day, in the 1870's, three men on horseback rode up and told him he had twenty-four hours to clear out or they'd remove him by force.

Just before sunrise the next day, my great-grandfather was waiting for them. As they came up to the house he began firing a huge, double-barrel shotgun right through the front door. The three intruders turned around in the darkness as fast as they could, dug their heels into their horses' flanks and never returned. He had never wanted to hit any of the gunmen. My great-grandfather just let them know that he meant business. Later on he became one of the most respected judges in the State of California.

I was born on September 11, 1918, in Long Beach, California during the last days of World War I. In a sense I was born into a new age, a dramatic period of history.

When I was less than one year old my first brother was born. It was an emotionally and physically draining time for my mother. The doctors had advised her to have an abortion but she decided, at great personal risk, to go ahead with the pregnancy. Because of the precarious balance of my mother's physical and emotional condition, I was sent to live with my maternal grandmother until I was four.

My grandmother had moved from her frontier ranch to Long Beach so my mother's younger sister and brother could receive an education. Tensions created by the cultural differences between her and my grandfather made their life together one of continual conflict. She was devout. When she was not working at home she was volunteering long hours of service in the Methodist Church. She was a master at organizing and cooking for the endless banquets and meetings. For the first years of my life I was always with her, and we never missed a Sunday morning or evening service at the old Grace Methodist Church in Long Beach. She paid strict attention to the sermon as I slept beside her in the pew.

There were definite rules by which the Christian lived and my value as a person depended upon how well I kept the rules. On these I was never to compromise. I felt a certain security in knowing the limits within which I would conduct my life.

When I returned to live with my family I was the oldest of four children. My father was a successful businessman who graduated from Columbia Law School. He had rebelled against the foregone conclusion that he was to go into the ministry. My Uncle John

Robinson stepped into the role. John Robinson graduated from the University of Southern California and the Harvard Divinity School, and was ordained as a Methodist minister. By the time he was thirty-nine he was the pastor of the Crescent Heights Methodist Church in Hollywood, California. He died tragically that year on Easter Sunday from pneumonia.

Throughout his life my father carried on an intellectual debate about God. We often spoke around the dinner table of the *universal spirit*, but he never discussed a personal relationship with the living Christ. He died on May 2, 1978, just before his ninetieth birthday. My wife Joan spent those last days at his bedside. His final statement to her was, "Yes dear, I really do believe." It had been a long questioning journey for him. Pop, as we called my father, gave us a questioning spirit. He also gave us his blessing to creatively pursue the world of position and achievement, but always within the moral and ethical context of the religious culture with which he had been ingrained.

My mother was an intellectual of great sensitivity and emotional need. She searched all her life for the truth. This search led her through metaphysics, psychology and analysis. Although her deep involvement seemed intense, to the point of negating the opportunity to just experience and celebrate life, we were encouraged to keep our personal doors open to intellectual investigation. This openness stimulated creative and differentiated life styles for all in my immediate family. My mother's constant theme was that each one of us had a totally different life to lead.

"Don't become like anyone else," she said. "Become what you want to be. That's where your integrity is. You have a potential to be nurtured. There is a purpose and an unique plan for your life." This was what individualism and fulfillment meant to her. She challenged us as we prepared to meet the opportunities and pressures of the world.

My mother confided in the last days of her life that Truth was to be found in the basic gospel she had learned as a child. "I've come full circle," she said. "You will understand this." Before she died I wrote her a letter in which I expressed the love I held for her. I thanked her for the guiding strength she had always provided. She died in peace, a committed Christian.

My brother, Charles Robinson was the president of the Marcona Corporation, a company that developed a large iron ore producing operation in Peru. To transport the iron ore, he founded the San Juan Carrier Corporation, the largest dry cargo shipping company in the world. These massive ships took their cargoes of iron ore from Peru through the Panama Canal and on to the great smelters on the East Coast. He resigned from these companies during the President Ford administration to become Deputy Secretary of State under Dr. Henry Kissinger. He now heads his own companies as president of Robinson Investments, Energy Transition Corporation, and Dyna Yacht Inc. of San Diego, California. His beautiful home is located on a hill overlooking Santa Fe, New Mexico.

My brother, Ted Robinson is a renowned golf course architect. He has designed many outstanding golf courses throughout the United States and the world, including a number in Palm Springs, California, Hawaii, Central America, Japan, Australia, and Indonesia. He received special recognition when his Sahallee golf course in Redmond, Washington was selected to host the PGA Championship in 1998. This is only the second time this prestigious event will be hosted in the Northwest United States.

My sister, Robin Jaqua raised a family of four, then earned her Ph.D. in psychology at the University of Oregon. Following her graduation she went to the Carl Jung Institute in Zurich, Switzerland, and is now a certified Jungian analyst. She established her practice and a training center in Eugene, Oregon. Her husband, John Jaqua, is one of the large stockholders and a member of the Board of Directors of the Nike Corporation, successful manufacturers of athletic equipment.

Within the dynamics of this family, I did develop a sense of value, stability, and belonging so essential to my personal development. Some of my lessons were learned quietly, the hard way. One morning, when I was only nine, we built a corral above the family ranch in the northern section of Los Angeles County. The corral was to be used for our summer roundup of the wild cattle on the mountain. I was sent to fill the canteens with water at a spring located over a mile away. The trail took me east along the top of Liebre Mountain to a hollow that formed the head of Cold Water Canyon. The open, treeless approach soon narrowed into a canyon of rock and giant live oaks. There, from a shadowed granite ledge, flowed a trickle of cold water through an open pipe and into a plank watering trough. It was a still and silent morning as I rode my buckskin horse into the darkness of the canyon. Then, suddenly, I heard the loud and penetrating scream of a wild animal. It was the unmistakable roar of a mountain lion. What a frightening moment it was, one I shall always remember as my first conscious experience of having to cope with fear. I hesitated. I was more afraid of going back to the men without the water than I was to proceed. I continued into the canyon, filled the canteens and returned to the corral. I never saw the lion, but clearly learned that one way to deal with fear was to meet it head on. Experience did teach many of us to negate our fears and I have an appreciation for how this happens.

My early drive was to fulfill my potential, the blueprint for my life. I would prove my value through personal accomplishment. This resulted in a rigidity and self-reliance that blocked deeper relationships with others and with the personal Christ. This is why my childhood was a paradox, being both a source of strength and weakness in establishing a philosophical base upon which I was to live out my life.

*   *   *   *

In 1933, I met Frank Buchman, who had generated world interest in a small group movement. This movement started in Oxford, England where groups of college students met together in intimate communities to share and listen for word and direction from God. Many years later this Oxford Group Movement became Moral Rearmament, a world movement.

In 1936, when I was seventeen, I took a train and went alone from Los Angeles to an international gathering of the Oxford Group Movement at Stockbridge, Massachusetts. This experience in the Berkshire Woods deeply influenced my spiritual and moral life. Frank Buchman and his movement provided the direction. He told us:

> *The only cure for confusion is to make God the decisive authority and to say yes to Him through the discipline of your life. Confusion comes from indecisiveness. Clarity comes from a positive moral change that illuminates the darkest motives and mobilizes latent powers. Absolute moral standards are the well spring of the inspired.*

I did have the feeling God was speaking to me, not in audible discourse but through a poetic style of revelation that I recorded in a notebook. I wanted to be His man in the fullest sense, and so committed my life to the highest of moral standards. This would establish, through action rather than words, the credibility I sought. I accepted Frank Buchman's yardstick: *absolute honesty, absolute love, absolute purity* and *absolute unselfishness*. I was committed to taking up the fight for an America that would become strong, clean and united; an America that would give a model of what the world longed to see. I had been given a vision, a comradeship and a plan to remake the world. It did not come out of an enlarged ego, but rather from the depths of idealism, a need to live out a deep purpose for my life, to be a part of something bigger than myself.

Positive feelings about my involvement with the Oxford Group Movement still remain with me. It provided important strength in the formative years of my life. At the same time, the experience created problems. It sent me on a tangent that delayed my personal encounter with Christ, for I measured my value as a person in direct relation to the degree I could meet the Oxford Groups standards of perfection. Rather than as guidelines for behavior, I accepted them as standards of measurement for human worth. I found myself caught in another system of legalism, and soon was falling short, experiencing confusion and continued loss of self-esteem.

Christ was my ethical standard of perfection, not my personal Savior. I struggled with this during my final years in high school and on into college. I met with superficial success, but was denied many relationships and avoided hard decisions that could not be measured by the yardstick I had adopted. These standards did a fair job in policing my life style. It was a self-imposed restriction, for my parents had given me much freedom in my personal life. It was a good thing as my hunger for adventure exposed me at an early age to some aspects of worldly life that could have been personally destructive had I not adopted this strict life style. In the deeper areas of my life I was not meeting the ethical and moral standards I wanted for myself. With this realization came a sense of guilt and isolation. The superficial rules were fairly easy for me to follow, but I was especially confused in the areas of absolute love and unselfishness. My love for others and myself depended upon a moral standard. I did not comprehend *unconditional love* in the psychological or theological sense. This lack of understanding created a barrier to my ever being effectively involved in a helping relationship.

*　　*　　*　　*

I entered the University of Southern California as a winner of a national competitive scholarship in 1937. The award was based on the outstanding record I had established in forensics and debate at Long Beach Polytechnic High School. I had learned the game well: research the subject, anticipate the challenge with forceful rebuttal, stick to the facts, keep my cool and hit hard when sensing a weakness in my opponent's argument. Many years later I was to learn that this was not the best formula for effective communication.

Two years later I left USC. It was the end of my sophomore year and I was experiencing an intense need to be immersed in a depth of living I was not getting in my academic studies. This was during the great depression and Alaska was the frontier. A high school friend and I purchased an eighteen-foot sailboat, christened it the Little Snark after the name of the ship in Jack London's book, and set sail for the north. I wanted to reflect on my life and gain a new perspective. After an adventurous summer voyage, I enrolled at the University of Alaska at Fairbanks. That was in the fall of 1939.

Hitler and his panzer divisions had moved with speed and force across the lowlands of Europe with callousness unmatched in history. This forced me to ask tough questions of myself. What part would God have me take should I be drafted for military service? What would be my decision? How would my decision measure up to an absolute standard of love? If I really believed in Christ as my ethical standard, could I ever be involved in the business of killing people? This became an overwhelming problem for me as the prospects for U.S. involvement in the war were coming closer to reality.

I completed a year and a half of undergraduate work at the University of Alaska. It was in the far North that I learned to fly. I was the first pilot in the Territory of Alaska to be trained under the Civilian Aeronautics government flight program. In January 1940, I soloed on skis and flew the wastelands before there was a single radio range with which to navigate. This was a time of high adventure at its best.

*   *   *   *

In 1940, I returned to USC to finish my degree in economics. It was a time of unrest, not to the degree experienced by the college generation of the Vietnam War, but nevertheless disturbing to those of us struggling for an ideological base for our lives.

At this time national leaders were debating the role the United States would take in the conflict which was developing with terrifying power across Europe. Some wanted greater military involvement, if not actual armed conflict. Others urged neutrality and isolation. It was an important debate and I felt strongly that those of us who would be inevitably thrown into combat had a right and responsibility to understand and discuss the issues involved.

One of the national leaders strongly supporting American involvement was Senator *Happy* Chandler from Kentucky. He came to USC, was greeted by the

President of the University and afforded the courtesy and recognition of the school.

Several weeks later the students invited Senator Gerald Nye of North Dakota to come and present his position on neutrality. He was a strong isolationist and his appearance aggravated the university officials. Some university official denied Senator Nye the courtesy of speaking in Bovard Auditorium where events of this kind were usually held. After the students circulated a petition, the Senator was allowed to speak in a small assembly hall at the law school. Not a single official greeted the Senator, and hundreds of students were turned away from the crowded assembly area.

I accepted this incident as a call to action and started a petition on campus calling for leadership that would support a more free discussion of the issues. It was directed to the President of the University. Hundreds of students signed the petition, not a daring thing today but in those days quite a step for students at a conservative university. When the petition had been completed, two other students and I took it to the editor of the Daily News, a Los Angeles newspaper with a more liberal orientation than the Los Angeles Times. They sent out a wire release. The next morning, news of the incident and the student reaction appeared in papers and news broadcasts across the United States.

I sent the original petition to the President of the University by registered mail. He had left town for several days, but I received the confirmation from the post office with his signature showing the delivery had been made. He never responded to the petition. A news release from his office to the media stated that an investigation indicated that subversive elements on the campus were responsible. That was me! I was a subversive! Ridiculous!

The school was in turmoil. Professors gathered in the student union at a 10:00 a.m. Chapel break, waving newspapers and carrying on heated discussions on both sides of the issue. My initial reaction was one of great anxiety. I believed suspension from the university was possible. I was angry that the issue was being discussed as "a subversive attempt to discredit the university by an element unsympathetic with the administrative leadership of the United States." That is what the newspapers had printed. I also felt stimulated. For three years I had attended classes and not more than three professors knew my name. Now I was a personality, and the recognition gave me a fresh sense of excitement.

There was never a confrontation or a discussion by the administration, with any of the students over this incident. I did meet with Asa Call the Chairman of the Board of Trustees, who was president of a large insurance company in Los Angeles. There in his impressive office I explained what had happened and why I felt so strongly about the issue.

"As students we should get both sides of a political issue, especially when the outcome could so directly impact our lives," I said. "I'm speaking for myself. I have no relation or connection with subversive groups who would like to discredit USC."

"You have nothing to fear," he stated very calmly. "I do not approve of the position the administration has taken."

"And if an issue should develop?" I waited for his

response with less anxiety than when I had first walked in to his office.

"I'll support your point of view."

My new position on campus did little to prepare me for what I would soon be volunteering to do. The escalating war would push abstract idealism out of the way and thrust the facts of life directly into my face. I would have to stand and choose to fight with the sword at my side, unsheathed.

It was a quiet Sunday morning, Dec. 7, 1941. I was having breakfast with my parents in our Long Beach home. As we ate, the almost unbelievable news came over the radio. Bombs had fallen on Pearl Harbor. We were at war with Japan.

I felt torn in different directions as I drove back to my room on campus. Graduation was less than two months away and I was acutely aware that this tragic turn in international events had changed the course of my life.

As a man becomes more mature in his search for God he gets a better understanding of when to act, when to retreat or when to just stand still and wait for clarity and direction. At this point in my spiritual development I saw no basis for discernment. I wanted to join the Navy, but if I did so I would not, could not, be within the limit of God's will. This was how I thought:

> *God forgive me. You know it's not in my nature to stand aside. It would be a violation of my very heritage, to the courage and strength I want so much to be a part of me. I can't be obligated to others who*

would engage in a fight for me and whose very lives would preserve the freedoms so important to me. I deny the standards to which I have committed my life, not the belief in the validity of the standards, but in my ability and willingness to live up to them in the tough decisions of my life. In my personal need to be honest with you, oh God, I do not ask for your blessing on this decision or personal protection in what I am about to do.

This was stilted, but in those days I was infected with deep idealism, not all bad, mind you, but one does grow more mellow over the years. It was a dark and lonely moment in my life for I desperately wanted to walk with God.

At 10:00 a.m. the following morning I volunteered for the Navy and began my training as a naval aviator. The experience eventually led to combat against the Empire of Japan in the far Pacific, and the escape from death as my plane exploded in the sea. After a long recuperation in Hawaii, I finally returned home to California.

My courtship and marriage to Joan during the war might have seemed impulsive to some. I have always accepted it as God-ordained. Her loyalty and strength of character would prove to be critical to me as I faced crisis after crisis while climbing to a teetering, unstable position on the pinnacle of success.

3

Getting started. . .Joan's story

It is with purpose that I backtrack on the story. Joan has been so entwined in the course of my life, that not putting our relationship in context would be an omission. In truth, without her, I am convinced, my journey would have taken an entirely different course.

Joan and I were married at the University Methodist Church in Seattle, Washington on March 4, 1943. Navy Air Squadron VC-31 was commissioned at the Sand Point Naval Air Station on Lake Washington. The pilots, now all new friends, came to our wedding. What a beautiful bride she was in the midst of all those navy dress uniforms. "I feel like a queen," she said. "Imagine, the only woman at my own wedding!"

Our commitment to one another came in rather a strange way. We had become acquainted when we were students at Polytechnic High School in Long Beach, California, but we had not dated in high school because she was three years younger than I. Joan was active and popular on campus and I was attracted to her vivacious personality and unusual beauty.

During my early college years at USC, I would drive back to Long Beach on the weekends and we dated periodically, but our relationship was never sustained. Although we both admitted an emotional attraction, our lives took different turns, mine to Alaska and then navy flight training, so we were not together for at least two years.

In January 1943, I was one of twelve new navy pilots sent to Norfolk, Virginia to qualify for aircraft carrier landings before being assigned to a fleet squadron. The British Aircraft carrier, H.M.S. Attacker was maneuvering in the winter Atlantic, waiting for the new pilots to land aboard. Each pilot was to make eight successful landings. Nine of us qualified that morning, but three were killed including Bob Koonze, who stalled directly ahead of me on his final landing approach. I have always believed that the plane spun in because there was a residue of ice left on the wings from a storm the night before. It was bitter cold. Bob was a fine pilot. There had to be a good reason for the accident other than just pilot error. Faulty catapult shots caused the other two deaths. Not enough pressure had been built up in the catapult to launch the planes with sufficient speed to fly. The pilots were just dumped into the sea in front of the carrier and were run over. None of the bodies were recovered.

That afternoon the base chaplain and I went to an old Norfolk rooming house where Bob's bride of twenty-nine days was waiting. "Bob was killed this morning," I said. She was shattered and collapsed in deep sobs. Later that evening I got on the train with her and began the long sorrow filled trip back to her home in Nebraska. Two days later her parents met us in Omaha. It was all so final. There was no body, no funeral, no nothing. I just told her good-bye and got back on the crowded lumbering train.

I moved westward over the fields of Nebraska, across the Continental Divide and then south through Salt Lake City to Las Vegas. Eventually I arrived in Los

Angeles. That long trip on the train gave me time to think. No longer could I take my existence for granted. Life was a temporary gift, precious in a way my adventurous spirit had not always perceived. The thought of going into combat without experiencing completeness, no matter how painful the eventual consequences, became unbearable. I wanted someone to love, someone who cared. It was something beyond reason. A godly voice within me said, *Go home again. Find Joan. Promise your life to the girl you love.* Those who have experienced wartime marriages will relate to what I tell. I found her working in a Long Beach bank.

Joan recalls, "They would hire anyone during the war. I knew nothing about banking and I had to learn fast. My salary was eighteen dollars a week and I felt fortunate to have a job. There I was a twenty-one year old teller when this young navy flyer walked in. He was handsome in his blue navy officer's uniform with those wings of gold."

"Robbie," she said, "What are you doing here?"

"Will you go to dinner with me?" I asked.

"When?"

"Tonight, if you can."

She worked until seven o'clock that evening because she had to reconcile the bankbooks before she could leave. We went directly to a quiet dinner and the visit we needed. Then it was time to go. I became very serious and looked right at her.

"Joan, I'm going to ask you a question, but I don't want you to answer it now. I will call you from Seattle in three days, and you can give me your answer then."

"What is the question?"

"Will you marry me?"

"Robbie!" She hesitated a moment to catch her breath. "This is a very unusual proposal, but I can't think about marrying you! I haven't seen you in two years."

"I understand. That's why I don't want you to answer me now."

I left immediately for Seattle and the Sand Point Naval Air Station in compliance with my orders to join the squadron. Three nights later I called Joan on the telephone.

"Yes, I will marry you," she said. "I was too surprised to say yes when you first asked me. But I do love you. I think I always have, and I will come."

A week later her parents took her to the train station in Los Angeles, a center of activity for emotional reunions and separations during the war. Joan had never been away from home before. "I was scared to death," she recalls. "Here I was, headed for Seattle to marry a man I loved and admired. But, did I really know him?"

I have always admired her courage, and her decision had taken courage. I saw it again when our squadron left San Diego on the aircraft carrier, Manila Bay, for the war with Japan. She stood on the dock waving good-bye. Then she returned to Long Beach to live with her parents until my return.

Joan describes her family as being poor, and I guess they were, but I never thought about that. She was born in Indiana and moved to California when she was seven weeks old. Her mother appeared strong, controlled and responsible. In fact, she was a very talented woman who suffered from the insecurities in her life. Out of this basic fear she found comfort and meaning in Christian Science. She was an excellent seamstress and earned extra income sewing for skaters in the Ice Follies.

In contrast, Joan says, her father was ineffective. "He was just a loving sensitive Irishman who could never get his act together. Basically, he lived in a fantasy world. I know now that it was his way of dealing with failure. He would just deny the reality of his life."

He did give Joan a lot of love and she responded to him. That was important. He was with her when in March 1944, the doorbell at their home rang and a Western Union delivery boy handed her a telegram. Joan later recalled:

"My world stopped. I knew, I just knew."

Trembling, she read the words:

> *We regret to inform you that your husband, Lt. F.W. Robinson, Jr. has been critically injured while in combat in the South Pacific. Please, do not divulge his ship or station. We will notify you when we receive more information.*

It was raining outside. The storm thrashed the palm trees and the shadows danced across the wet pavement. Joan and her father walked the streets of Long Beach that night, the rain washing her cheeks as the tears fell.

The days went by and there was no more word. Late in April she received a letter thoughtfully written by a nurse in Hawaii.

"Your husband is recovering in a base hospital here at Pearl Harbor."

After the war we began our family. We built a home in North Hollywood. By that time two of our children had been born, first our daughter Gail, and then our son Franklin Willard III. I started up the competitive ladder, for I did meet with continuing success as I took the competitive examinations for teaching and administrative positions within the Los Angeles Unified School District.

Joan was just thirty years old when we learned her mother had been suffering with breast cancer. Out of fear, her mother had kept her secret for four years. By the time we learned of the illness, the cancerous growth had progressed so far that we had no alternative but to support her. She had long before made the fatal decision not to seek medical treatment.

Joan, along with her father and sister, were not involved with Christian Science. But, the only loving thing we felt we could do now was to support her. Joan assumed the responsibility for taking her terminally ill mother to a Christian Science practitioner in Glendale until the time she was too weak to leave her bed. Every week, during her mother's long illness, Joan made the automobile trip with our two babies. She would leave early in the morning from North Hollywood to get her mother. They would make the long trip to Glendale, then back to Long Beach, returning to North Hollywood late in the afternoon. She did this for her mother without complaint.

These were hard and demanding years for both of us. I was working long hours as a teacher, coach and director of student activities at Canoga Park High School as well as continuing my graduate studies in the evening, forty miles away in downtown Los Angeles at USC.

In retrospect, I regret that I was not more sensitive to the deep emotional impact her mother's illness was having on Joan's life. Because of my insensitivity, I thought, then, that I was too busy to be with Joan when she was called to her mother's bed the day she slipped into a coma.

"I'm going to call that practitioner," Joan told her sister. "Maybe if he comes and sits by the bed she'll get some comfort." Joan quickly dialed his number.

"I can't come," he said. "I can do as much for her from here as I could if I came."

"But, think how humane it would be if you'd come and tell my mother you love her and pray for her," she argued.

"No, I can't do that."

"Then you're no damn good!" Joan shook with anger. "You're a fake and a phony! If you cared anything about her, and all the money she's paid you and the pain she's suffered to travel to see you, you'd at least give her the comfort of your presence."

"No, I won't come," he answered dispassionately.

Joan held her mother's hand as she died. She was left with a lot of bitterness over her mother's death. It was a bitterness she hadn't shared. Almost ten years later in a class at the Bel Air Presbyterian Church it all came out. Dr. Neil Warren, a Clinical Psychologist was teaching on the subject of death. He showed a film, which detailed, step by step, how a man and his family had dealt with his pending death from cancer. In the discussion that followed, someone said, "That's far fetched. It couldn't be like that. No one dies of cancer that way."

That tripped a backlog of anger in Joan. "You don't know what you're talking about," she screamed. She was very emotional and lost her self-control.

I didn't understand everything that was going on, but apparently it had to do with the rawness of her mother's death. I didn't know how to help her, and had little confidence in psychology.

Joan realized she needed help and talked with Dr. Warren on her own.

"Will you take me as a patient? I really need you," she pleaded.

Joan was in therapy with Dr. Warren for several months. He was the Dean of the School of Psychology at Fuller Seminary in Pasadena.

"My decision to go to Dr. Warren was the hardest and loneliest I had ever made on my own," Joan said, "but it was an important step on my journey to wholeness."

Shortly after my mother-in-law's death we moved to Tarzana, further west in the San Fernando Valley. Joan and I decided we should be involved in some church. After all, isn't this what good families do? And so we joined the St. James Presbyterian Church, which was just getting established, in our little community.

"Somehow I just never felt free to do this while my mother was living," Joan recalls, "But I met this wonderful little Scottish pastor, Calvin Duncan, and I responded to his sincerity and love for Christ. I asked him to baptize me."

For Joan to accept Christ at that time was more a

decision of the mind than a response to the Spirit. That is not exactly true either, but it explains the process, for God was initiating a relationship within her life which was to continue and grow over the years. Her confused religious background didn't help to make her relationship with the living Christ exceptionally clear. It would take time.

I completed my degrees through the doctorate and progressed up the expected promotional steps in teaching and administration. I served as assistant principal at Mark Twain Jr. High School in Venice, California, Assistant Principal and Principal of Reseda High and Principal of Airport Jr. High in Westchester, California. All these schools were within the rapidly expanding Los Angeles Unified School District.

Our youngest daughter, Dana, was born in June 1959. We had waited for her for eleven years and thought we'd never have another child. Gail was thirteen and Tri was eleven when Dana was born. She was a gift, a miracle. Our joy was shadowed by the serious infection that hit Joan, immediately following the birth. This necessitated a prolonged thirty-day stay in the hospital by Joan and our new little daughter. I remember vividly the day when a month after the birth, she for the first time held Dana in her arms. Joan cried with joy.

Two years later, because of Joan's continued poor health, she faced the reality of another major operation, a hysterectomy. She had a serious problem with adhesions as a result of her three previous major operations. This would complicate the operation. The afternoon following her surgery, Joan had a massive internal hemorrhage. Her blood pressure was gone. She had no pulse, no heartbeat. I was in the room alone with her when this happened. She could not speak.

"Get in here! There's something wrong," I yelled as I ran down the hospital corridor for help.

A team of medics, including the doctor who was on duty, rushed into the room with a lot of emergency medical apparatus. The hospital attendants attached wires to Joan's prone body and the doctor watched the dials on the machine with great intensity. In a moment I heard him say, "She's gone."

"No," I pleaded. "Keep working."

The doctor cut a gash in her leg, just above the ankle, and into her vein they pumped a massive blood transfusion. She began to respond. Another major operation that night saved her life.

Joan told me later, "I could hear everything that was going on in the room. When the doctor said, she's gone, I wanted to scream, No, I'm not gone! I'm here! Please, please keep working. Help me. My ears could still hear when nothing else in my body could respond."

Once more I had remained strong as I thought a Christian should, even if I didn't understand the fullness of His truth. It was a heavy responsibility to carry alone. I began teaching Sunday School classes and was elected an elder in the Presbyterian Church. Each Sunday I recited the Apostles' Creed. The services always raised theological questions and doubts within me, and I would often leave the sanctuary feeling I was a Christian pretender. I avoided communion because it didn't seem important, and I was uneasy with church ritual. Doing God's work in the world kept me busy, striving to please Him through legalism, church involvement and moral living. I was judgmental of myself and, in turn, of others. I was too busy and too much within myself to develop deep emotional ties and relationships.

My faith was a personal thing between God and me. I had no concept of belonging to the body of Christ or being a part of the vine as communicated in the Scriptures. What would it take to bring me into a relationship with the living Christ?

4

Beverley Hills High: I Arrive

On July 1, 1959 at the age of thirty-nine, I became the principal of Beverly Hills High School. I had worked hard, stuck my thumb into the pie and captured the plum. Popular surveys had rated Beverly Hills High School as one of the ten best in the country. That was the way it looked from the outside.

An unusual series of circumstances led to my arrival. On Easter Sunday afternoon of that year the phone rang in our Tarzana home.

I picked it up. "Hello."

"Could I speak with Dr. Robinson?"

"This is he," I said.

"I'm Ken Peters, Superintendent of Schools in Beverly Hills. I heard you speak at the State Administrative Conference in Sacramento and Dean Melbo at USC suggested I call you regarding the principalship at the high school."

"Yes," I said, "I was aware you were looking for a principal."

"Could we talk?" he asked.

The following Tuesday afternoon I went to Beverly Hills and met Superintendent Peters at the school.

Mr. Peters' call had not come as a surprise. Dr. Melbo, Dean of the School of Education, had called Joan and me to a conference at his office following the completion of my doctoral degree in administration. He encouraged us to extend our vision as far as my professional future was concerned.

"I know you feel secure about being a principal in Los Angeles, but keep the door open. There is opportunity out there if you have the courage to move, and I want to give you the assurance that USC will be behind you."

Dean Melbo talked again with me in a later meeting:

> *Don't be surprised if Ken Peters calls you. He is looking for a principal for Beverly Hills High School. Take a good look at it if it comes. There have been over fifty applications for that job, but Ken came in last week and said they still hadn't found the right man and did I have any suggestions? I told him they could look all over the country, but my recommendation would be to go right next door to Airport Junior High School. I told him about you and the special work you have accomplished in the administration and supervision of special programs for the gifted student. That carries a lot of weight in Beverly Hills. More importantly you have demonstrated that you can run a school.*

This was high praise from the Dean, and gave me the assurance I needed to even consider leaving the Los Angeles school system.

When I arrived in Beverly Hills for my initial conference with Ken Peters, I stepped for the first time on the campus that would be my professional home for the next seventeen years. The school was built in 1927 on a swelling of land at the western perimeter of the city. On a clear day one can see the length of Wilshire Boulevard, down through the Miracle Mile and beyond to the skyscrapers of downtown Los Angeles. To the northeast are the Hollywood Hills, and further on is the long sweep of the Sierra Madre mountains, often crowned in winter by the snow capped summit of Mt. Baldy. During my time at Beverly Hills, the towering buildings of Century City would emerge, casting their shadows across campus as the sun set quietly into the Pacific Ocean.

The High School is a masonry edifice of French-Norman architecture, roofed in red tile and crowned with a stately chime tower. It stretches majestically on the rise of land between Olympic and Santa Monica Boulevards. I climbed the long series of steps from Moreno Drive up to the entrance of the main building, pausing at the flagpole on my way to look at the broad lawns and back down over the landscaped terraces. The tall flagpole centered the campus. Here would be the focal point for the student demonstrations I would someday face. The office of the Principal was just inside the main entrance to the High School. "I have an appointment with Mr. Peters," I said to the receptionist.

"Yes, he is ready to see you."

Ken Peters looked the part for his position. He was a big man, handsome, with black wavy hair and a deep resonant voice commensurate with his imposing stature. I remember him as an upperclassman on the USC campus when he was captain of the national championship baseball team. He later played briefly for the St. Louis Cardinals. Here was a natural leader, intelligent, commanding, and in control. I sensed that immediately.

"Sit down," he said. It didn't take him long to get to the heart of our meeting.

"I don't know what you have heard about the school. We have a good program but we need to move ahead. Our Board is committed to a new era of excellence and I intend to build a staff that can produce the program we need. Not all our students are geniuses," he continued, "and yet in the name of excellence we are trying to put all of them through the same academic program."

"That does seem a little archaic," I said. "There is no testing and counseling program in place, no attempt to individualize student schedules, building around their interests and abilities?"

"That's the challenge. We have a lot to do."

Then he told me about the city. "Beverly Hills may not be the homogenous, gold-plated village it is said to be. Certainly there are large homes and mansions publicized around the world, but there are also very modest two-bedroom homes whose cost in the overly inflated southern California area is even that much more because of their Beverly Hills address. Living in Beverly Hills can mean, sharing a fifty-year-old duplex south of Wilshire Boulevard with one electrical outlet in the kitchen, or residing in one of those tremendous estates north of Sunset Boulevard."

"It is pretty well recognized that you have money to work with," I said.

"True. We have the lowest tax rate in the county, but the assessed valuation of the business property along Wilshire is so high we can sustain high per pupil costs in our program. We do have the resources."

It became increasingly apparent that an unusual opportunity was opening for me. "Can we talk about the specifics of the contract?" I asked. He gave me a salary figure.

"I'm not that concerned about the salary," I said. "Any time you start making drastic changes in a program, people get upset, and I need more than one year to prove I can do the job."

He paused for a moment. "The law controls this," he said. "We can never negotiate more than a year to year contract with a principal."

It was strange that the superintendent was allowed to enter into a multiple-year contract with the board, while the principal could only have a year to year contract. I accepted this reality, unaware that this system of hiring, when lethally mixed with the personalities of the superintendent and his board, would eventually threaten my career and bring me to a point of spiritual crisis.

Peters and I shook hands. "I want you to meet the board," he said. "This will be finalized at our next meeting." He was decisive and assuring, a good leader.

It didn't take long to learn the ins and the outs, the strengths and the idiosyncrasies of this complex educational institution. That was a key to survival. The superintendent had two assistants, one man in charge of personnel and another handled the business affairs of the district. Four eight-year elementary schools fed about 600 students into Beverly Hill's one high school each year. Incoming freshmen were already accustomed to specific teachers for specific subjects, having entered a departmentalized middle school concept in the sixth grade. In my sixteen and a half years as principal the student body grew from 1,700 to about 2,400.

On a day-to-day basis I was in charge of a certificated staff of about 150 persons, including teachers, librarians, nurses and counselors. Only four or five of these staff members actually lived in Beverly Hills. We couldn't afford to. In addition to the certificated staff, we had another 100 fulfilling other functions: plant maintenance, gardeners, cafeteria workers and secretaries.

During my tenure as principal I hired ninety-six percent of the staff that was in place at the time of my retirement. Recruiting these outstanding teachers took a large part of my time. To me it was an important responsibility. I would often go on long trips to interview prospective teachers. When I found the teacher I thought we needed, that person was encouraged to apply for a teaching position at Beverly Hills. The staff also assisted me in recruiting excellent faculty members in their particular discipline. I encouraged them to attend their professional meetings and to make contacts with other outstanding teachers. The board supported us in our efforts to secure the very best staff possible.

I organized the high school in the manner of a university, giving tremendous responsibility to the department heads. Since it was difficult for me to maintain personal contact with 150 teachers, we decided to form a Secondary Education Council. This group was composed of department heads and those with unique responsibilities, such as the head librarian, nurse and counselors.

I also held specific responsibility for the social studies, English, performing arts and the art departments with the assistant principals overseeing mathematics, science, foreign language, technical arts, business education and physical education. We would assist and guide the department heads.

A major share of my time was spent in crisis situations. I organized the school so I could move quickly into problem areas. My primary concern was with the staff and the students. An administrative assistant had the responsibility for the business aspects of running the school such as ordering supplies the supervision of non-certificated staff and the maintenance of the grounds and buildings.

Using this organizational approach I had time to involve the entire staff in developing the educational program for the school. This meant endless meetings with groups of teachers. Although no programs were forced upon the staff, our faculty was sensitive enough to the needs of individual students to change approaches when desirable.

Major crises would often arise with parents when they felt we were not responsive to their sons or daughters in a particular situation. Parents placed great emphasis on grades, and they would constantly contest a "B," "C" or "D" they thought was unfairly received. I tried, sometimes unsuccessfully, to explain to parents that teachers were the final authority on grades. Many parents could not or would not understand why I, as principal, did not exert my authority and assign a different grade. I couldn't do this legally even if I wanted to.

A few of our teachers, among some of the best we had in their subject matter background, had difficulty in relating to the students on a more personal or human level. This created problems for them in the classroom, problems they didn't understand when the students and parents became upset. It was a challenge to work effectively with these teachers.

We had a different problem in the drama department. Because of its excellent reputation and the unusual talent of our students, there was tremendous competition for roles in the school's productions. As soon as leads were selected I could expect disappointed parents to come barging into my office. They were emotional when their children lost out on a coveted role. It became such a problem that we established a committee with our department chairman and a drama teacher to set up procedures whereby they would explain to parents the basis for the decision that had been made. Many parents, with high aspirations for their children, simply didn't accept this. Our drama teacher, John Ingle, was a master of diplomacy as we worked through these issues with concerned parents.

Some problems were much more difficult. I have seen teachers completely distraught by a pupil's behavior. They would lose control and actually use physical force in their frustration. To touch a student in anger was never acceptable behavior, but almost understandable when one observed how far some would go in pressing a teacher in class. Such an action could face us with a lawsuit. I would do my best to resolve the unfortunate incident with the parents, while at the same time working with the teacher in searching for a more creative way to resolve conflict.

Another crisis situation could arise when a student accused a teacher of an immoral act. The teacher would deny it. Then the livid parent threatened to expose the incident. A teacher, now and then, was dismissed, but these were very difficult situations to determine. Lives were at stake and I wanted to be very careful.

The makeup of our student body would probably not fit the stereotype of the casual observer. Although approximately ninety percent of the students were Jewish by the time of my retirement, it was and still is a school in transition. Regardless, the students were far from all being the offspring of the elite, wealthy class that many people imagine. As I have explained, many lived in tiny homes or apartments with both parents working and struggling financially just to live in the Beverly Hills School District.

We began a program of admitting thirty minority students a year, most of them black, from outside the district. They entered as tenth graders so that we could work with them for three years. By the end of the third year about 100 were enrolled. This gave the school a positive input, something we needed even though community resistance would surface from time to time.

Several children of celebrities attended the school and, just as their schoolmates, some were very well adjusted and others created a constant problem. Some of the students reached celebrity status in their own right after graduation. Richard Dreyfuss was in the class of 1965. Bonnie Franklin, Rob Reiner and singer Shaun Cassidy were others from Beverly Hills High School who made it in the big time. Families living in our district placed great emphasis on education, and our students reflected this. We sent more students to the University of California than any other public high school in the State, about twenty-five percent of our graduating seniors. Approximately ninety-five percent of the graduates entered a school of higher education. It was an enviable record.

We gradually changed the educational structure of the school. We developed programs in team teaching, graded instruction on the basis of individual student ability, enriched elective opportunity, independent study, community work programs and modified flexible scheduling of the school day for students and teachers.

An expanded and modernized facility was needed to house this extensive new program. We went to the community in 1965 for approval of a ten million dollar bonding program. Ninety-five percent of the voters in the Beverly Hills District said, *yes*. With this emphatic statement of support and confidence we could move ahead with our ten million-dollar building program.

Year after year I became more firmly entrenched in my challenging profession. Problems arose and were solved. Crises would come and go, but generally I was satisfied and comfortable. I served on the YMCA board of directors, the education committee of the Beverly Hills Chamber of Commerce and was a member of the Beverly Hills Rotary Club. I enjoyed my prestigious position, humbly accepting praise for being a creative and dynamic administrator.

Then the students revolted. The strength of my roots could no longer fully support me and no show of authority could chase away the snowballing turmoil.

Hopefully, the background I have shared will help you understand my orientation as I faced the campus crises of the 1960's.

5

Moving Toward A Showdown

It happened in 1963 during a general school assembly: the first inkling of student rebellion at Beverly Hills High School. The students gathered in the school auditorium to hear the student council candidates for office make their nomination and acceptance speeches. The student council had appointed its own election committee. Under the supervision of the faculty advisor, the student leaders had determined the rules and the requirements for the campaign. All speeches were to be approved ahead of time, and any violation of the rules would disqualify a candidate. One after another, the candidates were nominated and each in turn gave their acceptance speech. They made their naive promises as they presented the platforms on which they ran. The listening students then applauded. Their applause was primarily based on the candidate's popularity.

Then Max came to the podium. He had been a quiet studious boy on campus. I did not know him.

"I am running for student body president," he began. "I know that what I'm about to say has not been approved, and I don't give a damn." There was an audible undertone throughout the assembly. "There's just too much domination by the administration in everything we do here. It's time we stood up and demanded a major role in running this school. After all, it's ours, not theirs!"

He was calling the students to arms. "We have demanding issues, and I will challenge the administration. If you elect me your student body president, student government will no longer be a rubber stamp for the principal. I promise you! The students are going to run this school." He was emotional and intense. He believed in what he was saying. He was not putting on a show to seek attention.

The students went wild and began cheering. Soon the assembly slipped into confusion. My reaction was one of amazement. I had never been faced with a direct challenge to administrative authority. It hit the faculty by surprise too. They wanted to see how I would respond. Students and faculty alike were waiting to see what would happen to Max. I thought of my own days as a student protester at USC. The issue was different here. Max had made it one of power, not of ideas. The very fabric of a great school had been threatened. I had no choice but to take decisive action.

I called Max into the office. "Sit down, Max. I am sorry this happened. I am disqualifying you from running for student body president. You know the rules. Further, you won't be allowed to attend classes until I meet with your parents." I was cool and collected. "Before you return, I need your assurance that in the future you will act responsibly. I want you and your parents to understand this. You knew the rules, and you made your own decision to disqualify yourself in the election."

I didn't officially suspend him, but he had challenged the school and my action hopefully would suffice as an appropriate administrative response. In my student days if you violated the basic school rules you took the consequences. During the revolt of the 1960's this was not always true.

Max brought his parents to school the next morning. His father, an upper level executive in the Xerox Corporation, and his mother, both supported their boy and his actions. Our conference ended in a stalemate of misunderstanding and frustration. I maneuvered out of the impasse by readmitting Max to class on probation, whatever that meant in this situation.

At no time did I reflect on the deep commitment I sensed in Max. What was at the bottom of his anger? I was deaf to his sincerity and concern. Max certainly wasn't acting out of a desire to be caught up in the emerging temper of the times, but out of a personal belief that there needed to be more student voice and involvement in the decision-making process. I never responded to that issue. Rather I came down on him and his parents with the need to adhere to the standards of the school. I was motivated by my deep sense of responsibility to the school and the community. I was the leader of the school, charged with the responsibility of maintaining the established procedures under which the school was to operate.

Sadly, after that Max and I never had anything but a negative relationship. Was my attitude too rigid? How should strong responsible leadership respond? Certainly, I was unprepared for the shaky years ahead.

The incident with Max was only the beginning. Other student activists, after consulting with the American Civil Liberties Union, brought their demands. The position taken by the Civil Liberties Union was that the school no longer had reasonable *parental authority* over the students when they were in school. The legal term *loco parentis* had historically established the accepted relationship between the teacher and the student. When the courts threw this concept out the window, student behavior deteriorated.

The activists first demanded more student freedom on campus. The dress code became a critical issue with students. The school district had a written policy that established the appropriate dress and grooming standard for students in the school district. The student leaders were smart and well advised. "You can't do anything about our demand," one aggressive leader yelled at me when I encountered him. "We are going directly to the members of the Board of Education. They are the ones who set the policy around here." They did go directly to the Board and won their demands.

This infuriated the superintendent, Ken Peters. He called me to his office.

"Get those kids under control. We can't have them running to the Board with their demands."

I tried to explain the complexity of the situation we faced.

"I understand that but it has to stop! There is just too much at stake. We can't build a program without community support, and I have had three calls today from leaders in the business community who want to know what's going on at the high school."

I knew he wasn't fooling. Seventy-five per cent of our financial support came from the highly assessed business properties in the district. But, the students had won a victory that fueled the fires of revolt. There would be more student demonstrations. Why couldn't Peters understand that?

I attempted to establish free speech areas away from the spectacular setting at the flagpole, but the student leaders would have no part of that. Exposure was what they wanted, and they had found the ideal location. The students would call the television stations prior to their rallies at the flagpole so they would have the news coverage they desired. Often these demonstrations were seen throughout the Los Angeles basin on the evening broadcasts.

Their demands expanded. The students wanted an extended elective program, less formal academic requirements and more flexibility in the educational program, issues, which I could partially support and upon which we were making progress.

Students wanted the freedom to smoke on campus. They wanted to leave campus without a permit, to literally come and go as they pleased. I was not willing to support these demands. On and on went our debates.

There was another interesting demand. The students wanted the right to attend other schools. Some felt they were living in a ghetto, even though it was a golden one. They said they wanted to know what the real world was like. I worked out an exchange program for them, but I had no takers, so the demand was dropped. I soon found that most were more interested in demonstrating than actually participating in any constructive solution. I was frustrated.

During this time, students at Roosevelt High School in Los Angeles went out on strike for *Chicano* rights. Our students held what you might call a sympathetic rally at the flagpole. A speaker from UCLA urged our students to march to Roosevelt High. This would show Beverly's compassion and give support to the Chicano cause, the unauthorized speaker said. Many students left campus and started walking east on Wilshire Boulevard. They had no concept of where they were going. Roosevelt High was twenty miles away in east L.A. and none of our students walked the distance. They just made their show along Wilshire Boulevard.

Gradually their demands became more focused on the issue of the Vietnam War. University students had recruited some of our most adamant young people to carry the fight to the high school. A few of these rebels actually planned to physically take over the school. Far fetched? Undercover agents had infiltrated the planning meeting held, of all places, in a room at the UCLA student union. This information came to us through the police and their undercover agents. We worked with the police, planning our response. Plain-clothes officers were with me constantly and we were in direct contact by portable radio with the Beverly Hills Police Department. Week after week, college rebel leaders urged our students to action. "Control Beverly," they said, "and we can control any high school in the State."

We planned our defense. Emergency lines of communication were established in case the activists cut telephone wires. Uniformed police were stationed near the school during the demonstrations, but they were not to be seen unless called because of the possibility of physical violence. The physical attack on the school never took place, perhaps because we were so well prepared to meet it. Other serious incidents did take place.

One day at noon a young adult appeared on campus and took over the microphone, which the protest leaders had provided. In vulgar and abusive language, he attacked the school, the government and society in general. One of the staff members panicked and independently called the police. When the officers arrived, a couple of hundred demonstrators ran down the broad steps fronting the flagpole, across Moreno Drive, and began to rock the patrol car in an attempt to turn it over. They were almost successful. It was violent! And all of this was right in front of Ken Peters' office. Eventually, the melee was brought under control, but not until the rebels were assured the speaker would not be arrested. No one was hurt, but it was a close call.

*   *   *   *

The responsibility for building an improved educational program during these times of tension became an increasing burden. The Superintendent of Schools, the Board of Education and the community were constantly evaluating me. Someone was at fault. It must be the high school administration and the administration was R-O-B-B-I-E   R-O-B-I-N-S-O-N. They would be swooping in for the kill.

I had stood up and faced the student protesters at every one of their demonstrations. Each time my response had been like that little boy, frightened by the scream of a mountain lion when sent for water in a dark remote canyon spring. Here again I had hidden behind a false front of assurance. The problem now was that this veneer was becoming brittle as it hardened.

As I felt myself being torn apart, I would flash back to other lessons I had learned. My parents had bought a ranch in the foothills of California's Antelope Valley when I was a small boy. I spent much time there with my grandfather whom I admired and loved. He gave me a horse and told me, "You will never break that animal if he thinks you're afraid of him. He'll sense your fear immediately. Control yourself and you will control your horse!"

The advice had worked again when I flew those bombing missions in the Pacific during World War II. In my initial experience in working with students this quiet and assured control was effective. But it was no longer working. I was experiencing continued feelings of loneliness, growing isolation and diminishing self-esteem. The strength of my grandfather's advice was failing me.

My relationship with the Superintendent of Schools was deteriorating. The qualities in his leadership style that I initially responded to as strength now intimidated me. I was angry. He demanded excellence and administrative control. His caustic memorandums ordering solutions to complex problems and signed, *Very truly yours, K.L. Peters, Superintendent of Schools,* became more frequent. Joan sensed my frustration and encouraged me to talk with her.

"Why do you just sit there and internalize your feelings? Kenny is a smart man and he knows how you feel. He is acting out of frustration and fear, too. You both are. If you want a relationship, confront him!"

"I can't do that. You have to play it *cool* with a man like Ken."

"Well, I just see that as a put-down. You are writing him off and that's not fair to a man of his stature."

"I knew you wouldn't understand," I shot back.

"Yes, I do understand. If you have a legitimate beef, fight it out if that is what you have to do. Just don't play games with one another. If I got one of those sarcastic memos I would march across the street and tell him to stick it in his ear! Do your job and tell him to get out of your hair. I like Kenny and down deep you do too. You don't let someone you like run all over you." Joan was wound up!

"No, I can't do that. I'm not going to let him know he is getting to me. That would be the last way to handle Kenneth L. Peters." It was time to tone down this conversation.

*   *   *   *

Let me introduce three unusual personalities who play a dominant role in the story I tell.

The first is Richard Keelor, head football coach and athletic director. We had a dismal sports program. It needed pumping up. I hired Dick Keelor from Long Beach Polytechnic High School for the task. He was confident in his own ability and imbued confidence in others. He did the job. He became a dominant personality and an effective support in the showdown I would face.

My relationship with Kully Rabkin was different. Kully was teaching English at Montebello High School and wanted to join the Beverly Hills faculty. I knew he was an outstanding teacher, but he had a volatile personality. We didn't need any more *prima donnas* on the faculty. It was against my better judgment at the time that I recommended Kully for a contract. Looking back, I recognize that a deeper intuition overrode my initial judgment. It took three years from the time he applied until we offered Kully a contract. He was a Russian Jew who began his teaching in Canada and later became a citizen of the United States.

As principal, I was required to make regular visits to the classrooms so I would have some basis for the official evaluations of a teacher. I visited Kully's class. He was a creative teacher and the lesson came alive. I left, but returned to his room at the close of school.

"Kully, I needed to come back and tell you how much I enjoyed your class. It was a great lesson. I wish I could be one of your students."

He was silent for a moment.

"Robbie," he said, "This is the first time in all my years of teaching that anyone has told me directly that I was a good teacher."

In 1966 I recommended Kully to be Chairman of the English Department. I went into the relationship with my eyes wide open. The rumors I had heard about his fiery personality before he joined Beverly had been confirmed on several occasions. It was inevitable that we would have conflict, but by some strange mixture in our diverse personalities we were able to relate and deal with one another with respect.

"You're cutting the legs out from under our department," he would scream. "Some of our teachers have over a hundred students a day in their five classes. How can a teacher correct that many papers?"

"I know, Kully, but you have to stay in balance with the rest of the departments."

"Not in English," he retorted.

"Look, I accept that you're only going to be as good a department chairman as you are supportive of the members of your department. You are their representative, the liaison with the administration. It's your duty and responsibility to bring the concerns of the department to the administration. You are able to do that, and you are a good chairman. Just because I can't give everything you demand, doesn't make one snap of difference in my feeling about you."

Kully seemed to feel the same way. Our friendship continued to grow and never wavered. He became my confidant.

"Kully, I don't know what to do about all this turmoil. We need to make some changes, but we can't give the school away in the process. I know clamping down, putting on tight restrictions is the worst thing we could do."

"I see a change in you, Robbie. You probably don't even see it in yourself. You used to be more authoritative and you don't seem so sure of yourself any more. I personally like that but some are going to see it as a weakness." He laughed. "You need to be a better politician in this district."

He became serious. "You are being misunderstood. Here is the way I see it. You have the capacity to choose the right people and delegate to them the authority to do their job. You make good judgments about character and you are willing to experiment and make mistakes. I feel important because of the way you treat me. Part of the problem is that people don't really have a chance to know you."

I was able to talk to Kully Rabkin.

Lyle was another story. Lyle is black, although I have never thought of him primarily in this way. He had been an art teacher at Mark Twain Junior High in Venice. He was a talented artist in his own right, but more important he loved kids and worked with the students regardless of their natural talent. We needed this added dimension in our art program.

"Lyle," I said, in our initial conference. "I want you to come to Beverly. Do you think you can take it? There are a lot of pressures here."

"What do you mean?"

"I mean we have a program that is great for the talented art student, but I would like to see more of our people involved. That means a change in philosophy that will create tensions within the art department."

"I can handle that," he responded.

"And, there is something else."

"What?"

"You will be the first black on the faculty. The school is ready for that, but I wanted to be up front with you."

"I've been there before, I can handle it."

*   *   *   *

The students continued their demonstrations against the Vietnam War. Following the news that several student demonstrators had been killed by State militiamen at Kent State University, a massive demonstration of protest developed on our campus. During the morning break they came again to the flagpole. The gathering started slowly, but soon the protesters broke out their sound system, and an off campus speaker arrived. Things began to heat up as he spoke. Others, mostly our own students, became emotional and grabbed the microphone. They denounced the United States government with threats and obscenities. I moved among the heated throng, trying as best I could to calm the situation. Looking up the staircase by the school auditorium I saw Lyle Suter recording the demonstration on audiotape and film. He was one of the few staff members who was willing to venture forth during the demonstrations. Later I went to him.

"Lyle, I know you recorded the demonstration this morning."

"Yes."

"That's great. I would like to get a copy so I can show the film to the Board of Education. They need to know first hand what is going on."

Lyle thought he was being used as a spy to trap the students. A letter from him was on my desk the next morning.

> *Dear Dr. Robinson,*
>
> *Under no circumstances will I turn the film of the demonstration over to you. I feel I am being used to trap the students. This is not ethical. Further, I do not have the film in my possession at this time, and I don't know where it is.*
>
> *Sincerely yours,*
> *Lyle Suter*

Lyle found out later that one of his student helpers had taken the film to the audiovisual department to make an extra copy. Lyle stormed into the duplicating room, grabbed it off the machine, and to the surprise of the student and the teacher, ran off with the film. He told me later, "I was prepared to be fired for insubordination." He waited at his home, but no one called him. No one said anything. Finally, I called him into the office for another reason.

"The Art Department chairmanship is open," I said. "I know you are interested."

"Yes," he answered, somewhat taken by surprise. "I can do a good job."

"You've had difficulty dealing with authority," I continued. "You don't adhere to policy, you miss deadlines in making your reports and you can't stay within your budget." He knew all of this was true. "I'll be on your back every time you *goof* up. Could you take that?" The conversation was not quite that abrupt, but Lyle got the message.

"Yes, I think I can."

"O.K., Lyle, I'm recommending you for the position." Lyle knew I would be criticized for giving him the job. But I wanted to take the chance. He had a basic integrity I admired. He didn't play games with me and I always knew where he stood.

*   *   *   *

Through those years of campus unrest and social upheaval, there were times when I tried to dig deeper into my own resources for support and strength. But still in many of my personal interactions with students and staff I became increasingly ineffective. On the outside I would smile but on the inside I was in pain. I would need help.

6

Struggle To Emerge

As my inner tension grew I became more and more closed to others. I questioned myself, afraid that if this insecurity showed I would lose control. In this confusion, I periodically felt compelled to show a little more old fashioned force.

I remember one confrontation with the staff in which I didn't practice any of the basic rules of good human relations. It was a disaster. An assistant principal reported that the counselors had rejected a request to help supervise the school during demonstrations. They thought it would damage their image with the students. I called a special meeting and confronted them about their lack of cooperation and unwillingness to help. I was hostile, aggressive and assertive. When I finished I asked them to respond. One of the young women counselors began to cry. Another was speechless and the rest seemed unwilling to engage in a productive discussion of the issues involved. I had destroyed any possibility for meaningful communication. A much-needed positive understanding between the counseling staff and myself was out of reach. It was apparent that this style of confrontation was counter productive in establishing the environment I inherently wanted to build. Yet it was precisely this type of encounter I would be forced to attend.

The *Monte Corona Adventure* as we called it was a

purely humanistic attempt on the part of the Beverly Hills Unified School District to train teachers and administrators to become more effective in their relationships. It was an experience in *Sensitivity Training* that was in vogue in the 1960's.

Several members of the Board proposed that district personnel participate in this program of *Sensitivity Training*. Participation was voluntary, although the Assistant Superintendent advised me that if I wanted my contract renewed the following year it would be wise to attend.

I had always had an innate fear of disclosing myself. That would be forfeiting my privacy. Participation in personal group dynamics gave me feelings that bordered on terror. It was with great reluctance that on a Friday afternoon I boarded the chartered bus and left Los Angeles for Monte Corona, a small conference center near Lake Arrowhead. For two strenuous days we were involved. Imported leaders tried their best to force us into confrontation with one another. My group leader used many psychological gimmicks in his attempt to put us in a position of emotional exposure and vulnerability. If someone broke, his mission was accomplished!

I remember one talented teacher who on occasion was insensitive. This was because he was so focused and hard working that it appeared to some that he didn't give a flip for others. He just had never given the time to establish a relationship with his colleagues. I had gone to great lengths to recruit him from another outstanding high school in the area, because I knew he could bring excellence to an important area in the educational program.

The leader of the facilitating team group immediately detected the teacher's weakness, never understanding his tremendous strengths and dedication. In the name of honesty he ripped him apart, stripping him down before the entire group. Naturally, the teacher was defensive. He bragged about this ability as a teacher and the status he had achieved.

This antagonized others in the group and the leader saw his opening. "You're an egotistical bastard," he yelled. "You won't listen to anyone else! You have no sensitivity! I doubt that you have one decent relationship in your life."

The teacher's face began to glow. The redness rose. As he struggled to respond, he ran his fingers through his gray hair. He fidgeted with his glasses. Then he fought back. "I'm well established in my profession. I have as good a background and experience in my field as anyone you will ever meet. I know where I'm at. I resent what is going on here.

"Your frustrating me," the leader retorted. "You're not hearing me. You don't know where you're at. That's the problem!" The facilitator smiled, nodded and then smirked as if disgusted. "The only thing you're proving." He said evenly, "is your egotism."

This went on for about twenty minutes and the others became jittery. One teacher tried to pour oil on the water.

"There might be some truth in what you're telling him, but is there a better way of handling it? Is this dialogue really constructive?"

Most of us were scared and didn't say anything; self-protection was our main interest. But truthfully, I was sick at heart for my colleague. It was impossible now to bring any understanding or healing to the situation.

Before the weekend was over I saw some of my associates dropping protective barriers. Some were less inhibited than I had ever seen them, but not necessarily in a positive way. The use of profanity and vulgarity increased for shock value. "I'm free to be me," was the message.

Most of the interaction was in small groups with the administrators and supervisors separated from the teachers. There were a couple of sessions, however, where general school policy was discussed. In one of these sessions the district policy on the hiring of teachers came up.

"How do you, where do you find qualified black teachers?" I asked.

Lyle Suter shot back "I know it's bad to be emotional but I am emotional."

It was apparent he was ready to explode.

On one side of him was the President of the Board of Education, a woman and former radio actress who had played the part of Jewel on the original Amos and Andy show. This added an unspoken dynamic to the discussion. On the other side of Lyle was Ken Peters. Ken reached over and held Lyle's arm in a restraining gesture. It was an attempt to protect Lyle and not let him get carried away in the presence of the board member.

Lyle yelled, "You can't make me keep quiet. Let me answer Robbie. You're not in this Peters."

The superintendent moved away, giving Lyle a withering stare. Lyle got wound up.

"Robbie, you live out in the sterile San Fernando Valley, surrounding yourself with white Christian Protestants. All this district wants is a nice Negro guy who went to college and has closely cropped hair and wears a shirt and tie. You think a nice Negro doesn't make waves

Lyle deliberately used the word *Negro* to accuse us of thinking *Negro*, a complacent Uncle Tom, rather than as an emerging Black, establishing his own identity.

"You don't come in contact with us, Robbie, so you don't know where to find qualified black people. Damn it, would you hire a qualified chemistry teacher if he had a big natural?"

I never had a chance to answer as the superintendent took over.

"We don't have to listen to this vulgar, crude talk."

With that, Nate Jackson, a powerful and dynamic black man who was a member of the outside enabling team took over with emotion.

"Man, I want you to know I'm right here on the same level doing my brother's thing right along here beside him." It didn't make a lot of sense, but emotions were high.

"Mr. Peters I resent you putting Lyle down like this," added an elementary school teacher.

Nate, the teacher and others gave Lyle the support to push his point.

That night Lyle and several other teachers barged in, uninvited, and sat down on the floor of the cabin where the administrative team was meeting.

"We're here to talk," Lyle began, "We don't want to be separated anymore."

I couldn't believe what I was seeing. Ken's angry eyes found Lyle, but Lyle continued.

"Mr. Peters, I want you to know that I do not hold you in awe even though you are a good administrator. I think of you as just another man."

Another person used the word *manipulative* to describe the relationship between the faculty and administration. When Peters heard the word *manipulative* he became angrier.

"I resent this intrusion. This is why we want our groups separated. I'm leaving!"

Later, Lyle colorfully described the incident.

"Kenny just picked up his sneakers in one hand, his little bag in the other hand and walked out." He also told me, "I wanted to get far away from all of you. I hated you. I felt cheated because from the moment we arrived we were segregated into groups of teachers and administrators except when we were to talk about impersonal policy issues. We weren't allowed to sit and rap, just person to person. I felt degraded. I wanted to get far away."

For me the experience at Monte Corona was negative but it did provoke a lot of thought. After I returned home Sunday afternoon, Joan and I sat in our patio. We talked late into the night about what happened. I described the interaction, the things the people did and what they said.

"I need to know more about emotions. If this is what is going on in the world of psychology I'm afraid of it."

"It is just like everything else," she responded. "There is both good and bad in Psychology. We just need to differentiate between the two and use what is good."

I am aware of two developments, which took place in me as a result of the Monte Corona experience. One was negative as I continued to confront people in ways, which were neither creative nor helpful. There is a place for confrontation, but as I learned later, it is usually harmful unless a deep level of trust and respect has been established between those involved. The lack of trust was one reason my meeting with the school counselors had been so destructive.

I later learned to force clarification when I felt a discrepancy between what a person said they were feeling and what their actions demonstrated. Confrontation is necessary at times for growth to occur, but means so much more when it is surrounded by trust and understanding. I still experience creative confrontation as the most difficult aspect of the helping relationship.

The second thing that developed in me as a result of the Monte Corona experience was the beginning of awareness that others also experienced aloneness and a deep need to become whole. I sensed that I did not really know my closest colleagues and that many of our interactions were not very honest. How could I become free to experience a deeper fullness of life? It became increasingly evident that the protective barriers between myself and others needed to be broken down, but within a context which took the feelings of others into account.

I had seen the damage inherent in a more open way of relating where love and caring were not the primary motivations for building a relationship. The human personality is frail and can be damaged in the name of emancipation. I began to see human personality as a larva in its beginning stage: immature, wingless, often in a wormlike form, a protective cocoon enveloping it. This protection is important to growth, but just as important is its struggle to emerge into a fuller expression of life in beauty and flight.

Nature does not break new life from the cocoon. Gradually, in the process of life, nurtured in the softness of spring, impetus comes from within and soon a new and beautiful life breaks forth. Shouldn't human personality, as such an important part of nature, be treated with such care? What were the forces within human relationships, which could nurture a person's emergence into fullness? What kind of death must I undergo before I can emerge? Secular culture was telling me a fuller life came through humanistic techniques. I began to sense that this was a betrayal of God's creation and the spiritual pulsation of life itself that might bring fuller meaning to my world.

I had a deepening sense of need for a spiritual dimension in human relationships, yes even to the point of commitment to the reality of the Christian vision. But how? I was a lonely, frightened person, responding ineffectively to others in this imperfect world. Monte Corona had shown me that. I wanted to connect and experience a love that would respond to the bleeding wounds of the human situation, one that would heal me and others. I wanted to be free of a judgmental nature that separated me from others. My philosophical speculation turned into dramatic reality as I neared a crisis in my leadership of the school.

7

A Time To Fight Or Fade

Educational leaders everywhere went through crises during this rebellious period in American education. Some survived because of their charisma and basic popularity. Others retired early or assumed different positions. In rare occasions administrators modified their style and became effective leaders.

It became painfully apparent that changes would have to take place in me if I were to survive these tumultuous times. The *strong benevolent leader* would never describe me, and that wouldn't work now anyway. I had tried to be responsible, fair, and decisive when I thought the situation demanded that kind of strength, but that wasn't working either. I was committed to and felt most comfortable in a participatory leadership style, one that involved others in decision making and deliberately sought the individual and his unique strengths. But I was experiencing growing confusion and doubt regarding effective leadership styles. Greater participation in decision-making on the part of the various groups within the school during times of crises was contributing to confusion rather than solution.

An arbitrary display of power was equally counterproductive. Flexibility in leadership was demanded, but where was the line to be drawn between authority and participation in the fluid issues that came in wave after wave?

The faculty was divided on philosophy and

approach. Some expressed the need for decision by ultimatum. For them the desperation of the times demanded more of an authoritative attack through administrative strength. For many of the younger teachers the need was for a more responsive leadership. They wanted to involve larger segments of the school community in decision making. They wanted change accomplished at a faster pace. *We need to make the school more relevant.* I heard that word *relevant* over and over again. They gave tacit support to the student leaders and encouraged them to confront the issues that concerned them. There were many subtle ways in which they supported militant young people to act out the frustrations they were not willing to act upon themselves.

We played insidious games, which negated the building of trust and the conditions for healing. Openness became increasingly difficult and I found myself withdrawing from confrontation and meaningful involvement. I learned to protect myself, but this compounded my feelings of inadequacy and ineffectiveness. I had been so success-oriented that failure was unthinkable. Yet, failure was becoming a strong possibility. I reacted with a self-preservation instinct.

I found myself employing the very techniques that increased the possibility of failure. I put psychological blocks on my creative abilities. All of my efforts were directed at protecting my position, rather than exercising my unique gift from God in creative administration. I desperately needed to be freed for new styles of leadership. I was painfully aware of my need, but at a loss as to how to change. I was experiencing *crisis in leadership*.

* * * *

The doors that opened to new insights came from unexpected sources and were an important part of my search for wholeness, which could evoke the healing so desperately needed in my relationships at Beverly Hills High School. Suddenly, unexpectedly, it took a death to teach me a lesson about life.

Dave was the principal at Horace Mann Elementary School. He was in his late thirties, an athletic five feet ten inches in height. He usually wore a brown business suit and tie and puffed on his pipe during staff meetings. He gave the impression he was very well composed, a cool character who was adequate to any situation. He had been a baseball player at USC and carried the confidence of a winning team with him. His answer to any question was very deliberate, thoughtful and controlled. He was in complete charge of himself, enjoyed his membership in the Playboy Club and appeared happy after his second marriage.

District staff meetings were held twice a month around a long walnut table in an upper-level conference room. The superintendent always sat at the center of one side of the long table. The high school principal, the four elementary school principals and the district supervisors and administrators found their places around the rest of the table.

There were no assigned places, but over a period of time we established our own seating order. I sat to the left of Ken Peters, with Dave directly across from me.

There we sat, year after year, playing our administrative roles, protecting ourselves and secretly feeling relieved when someone else was in a defensive position. It was a Friday morning. I entered the conference room a few minutes early, poured myself a cup of coffee and then took my usual place at the table.

"How goes it?" I asked Dave.

He didn't answer at first, swallowed some coffee and then responded in a rather off-hand manner.

"Oh, pretty well, I guess."

Today I would hear this response as a timid risk from someone in need. Back then I neither heard nor cared to hear. A typical two-hour staff meeting followed and we left for our respective schools.

That night, alone in his apartment, Dave took a pistol and shot himself through the head. A personal hand-written note outlined in detail the deep personal pain he had been experiencing.

Why hadn't I been able to hear and respond to his faint cry for help? As leaders in the district we continually gave lip service to the need for establishing a sensitive and caring climate in which to build better relationships within the schools. Yet even at the staff level, perhaps even more dramatically at the staff level, we were destitute when it came to knowing how to develop a trusting and caring attitude with one another. We couldn't live a life style, which modeled the very thing we most wanted between teachers and students.

It took the suicidal death of a young man I loosely called *friend* to motivate a deeper search for my own humanness. I do not harbor the illusion that I could have personally deterred his action. Yet I have learned to take the threat of suicide seriously and know the importance of continued conversation until professional help becomes available. No longer will I willingly or unwillingly avoid emotional involvement with someone in pain. This tragic incident drove home my need to be more sensitive to those around me.

*   *   *   *

I began to get inklings that there was a growing division on the board over the question of my effectiveness as principal of the high school. You would have had to be blind not to see that the board was dividing philosophically over a number of issues. The majority, including the president, voted in what was being identified as the liberal block. The remaining two members represented a more moderate point of view and were generally more supportive of the administrative leadership within the district.

As the students became more aggressive and their demands were turned down at the school level, they continued going directly to the board, as in the dress code issue. Student militant leadership was sophisticated and they knew where the source of power rested when it came to establishing policy. This infuriated the board members who prided themselves on running the district in good order. Also, as tension increased on campus, members of the faculty, dissatisfied with my leadership, went directly to the liberal board members. This was the beginning of an effort to remove me as the principal of the high school.

During the final two weeks of February 1970, Ken Peters called me to his office.

"I hate to tell you this," he said, "but it's my responsibility as superintendent. The Board of Education, in a closed personnel session, has voted two to three to terminate you as principal of the high school as of June 30th. They realize you have tenure as a teacher in the district and so rather than to fire you as principal they are willing to give you another assignment in the district office." Peters went on, "I advise you to take it, although I'll certainly support you in whatever decision you make."

My official evaluations had always been excellent, but the news didn't shock me. The turmoil had been too great.

"Tell me," I asked, keeping my professional voice firm and level, "what is the board's main objection to me?"

"The majority feels *we're* not sensitive to students in view of changing times. They would have this district in chaos if they had their way. They don't know what trouble is, but they control the majority vote. Unfortunately, you're the one, as principal, with the yearly contract."

I appreciated his including himself in the issue with the board by saying *we're* not sensitive. There was always this paradox in our relationship.

Ken Peters stood by the door of his office. "I'll give you twenty-four hours to let me know whether you want to resign and take another job in the district or fight this thing and face being fired. I think it would be a mistake not to take the new assignment, but I'll back you up in whatever you decide. They are required to give you a personnel hearing before taking official action."

I left the office and hurried back to the high school. I needed to get my thoughts together. It was time to fight for my job or fade into an obscure web of paper-pushing spiders chasing after dead flies. Perhaps the Board was right and it was only my ego getting in the way. After all, the faculty was polarized, the community seemed confused, the Board was split and the student activists were in rebellion. I had tried to be an effective communicator, but every time I came out to do something, I got hit on the head. It was true that I was drawing tighter into my shell, playing my cards, as they say, closer to my belt. Why not? I tried to put up a good front, to show I was still in control. But I didn't know how to deal with it. I was confused. Was this an issue worth facing? Did I even have a chance? Call it ego. Call it stubbornness. I don't know. But down deep inside, the answer was there. I could not just quit.

The next day I walked into Ken Peter's office with my decision. "I came as principal and when I go from this district I will leave as principal. I would rather do that than be bought off with a new assignment that has no real validity at all."

"I'll accept that, even though I think you're committing professional suicide. Your only hope will be the defeat of the incumbent board in the coming election. No one has ever done that."

Peters and I quickly shook hands and I left, determined to summon all the Robinson grit within me and not give up until the last vote had been counted. In a few months the Board would be up for reelection. If the personnel changed dramatically enough I had a chance to be reinstated as principal should their expected action against me actually take place.

I needed to talk with someone at school. Kully was my friend, the one who would understand. Often we would go out on the school track and Kully would walk four or five laps with me as I warmed down from the three miles I regularly jogged. We had continued to develop a close and trusting relationship.

"Kully, the board has decided to terminate my contract at their next meeting."

"They're going to do what?"

"Yes, Peters called me in and gave me the word."

I reviewed all that had gone on.

"Actually, I don't have any real options, but I did tell Peters they would have to fire me."

"Well, I'm going to ask the faculty president to call a meeting of the Secondary Education Council. I'm going to get to the bottom of this. Too many people think they have easy answers to complex problems."

He seemed so upset. He was so concerned.

Two days later I was summoned before the Secondary Education Council, the governing body we had organized. It was composed of faculty officers, department heads and school administrators. I was asked to relate my view of the Board's charges against me and the procedure it had followed in dealing with me. Step by step, I reviewed my conferences with the Superintendent, my official evaluations and the situation, as I perceived it. No one took issue; no one questioned me.

The Secondary Education Council then decided to ask for a meeting with the Board. They drafted a telegram in support of me and Kully was selected as spokesman for the Council. He signed his name to the telegram, listing his home telephone number as the means to respond. The telegram was sent to each member of the Board at four o'clock that afternoon. By 6:30 p.m. every member of the Board had called Kully. All were upset over the telegram. They told him this was no way to proceed, that communication should go through the Superintendent. By this time Peters was furious. He wanted to be the one in control. It was too late for any of us to retreat, and anyway I had not known of the action until Peters confronted me!

The following Monday afternoon the Superintendent, as the official representative for the Board, appeared before the Secondary Education Council. He came well prepared with his folders documenting every meeting he or the Board ever had with me. Dates and times of even our most informal meetings were there as a matter of record.

I had always had an instinct for caution in previous meetings with the Superintendent. My instincts had been right. He was cool, matter-of-fact and very impersonal. It was apparent the situation had gone too far by this time to expect significant support from him. He was the Superintendent. The man in control.

The Secondary Education Council went into closed session. Kully Rabkin told me later that it was a wild session. A number of the members began attacking me.

Kully had been livid with anger. "If you've got to criticize him, do it to his face. You're dishonest and you're trying to railroad him because you think he's down."

Dick Keelor, head of the boys' physical education

department and the Director of Athletics had jumped in, Kully told me.

"By God, this is the time to back him. He's always backed us."

A vote was finally held, and the Council went on official record to the Board with a vote of confidence for me, although it was far from unanimous.

I drove home and told Joan what had happened. There was no way I could isolate her from the battle or keep her from the war. She always knew what was going on with me even when I wasn't sure myself. It would not be an easy time for our family.

Our oldest daughter, Gail, had just been married. While her husband was finishing medical school at UCLA, she was teaching first grade at Beverly Vista, one of the elementary schools in the Beverly Hills Unified School District.

"The teachers are supportive and sympathetic, but it is awkward," she said. "They know you are in a crossfire, but they seem embarrassed because they are convinced of your impending fate."

Gail felt somewhat isolated because the teachers around her didn't know what to say and that made all of them uncomfortable. Most knew I was her father, even though she now had a different last name.

Night after night I would come home from school and Joan and I would talk. I reviewed the events of the day.

"It is so hard to lead a school when you are just waiting for that meeting with the Board. The ax is going to fall. I wish the hearing were over." I spoke with a lot of tension. "How much longer can I take it?"

"Why don't you talk with Ken Peters again?" Joan asked. "You know, I'd...I'd..." The anger would well up within her. "Why don't you talk with the leaders in the community. You have a lot of friends, a lot of support."

"I don't want to talk to the community. If they can't see how superior the educational program in the school is, regardless of the trouble, then all the talking in the world will do no good."

I was defensive and feeling sorry for myself. I was becoming aware of the same thing Gail was, but at an almost unconscious level. Why were so few on the staff openly supportive of me? Many I counted as friends just seemed to be fading into the walls. They were simply disappearing. All of this was very painful.

*　　*　　*　　*

There were a few bright spots. One came from the black students in the school. Lyle Suter was their sponsor. They stormed the office one noon. What crisis now? Before I could gain equilibrium they placed a black natural wig on my head, dark glasses over my eyes and a Somali blanket over my shoulders.

"We want you to be our black brother," their leader said.

Right there in the office they did make me their black brother and gave me a birth certificate and the handshake to prove it. Laughter and tears! I went around the room, mutually embracing with spontaneous and healing love. This encounter has remained special to me. To this day I think of Lyle as my *brother*.

* * * *

The few bright spots had little effect on the forces determined to get rid of me. They were adamant that I was an ineffective administrator, not communicating with the students and the job was getting beyond my control. There was enough truth to the charges that they were able to build their case even though the positive new educational programs in the school were apparent. That should have been obvious to the most casual observer. But they were frustrating times, and the majority of the Board and those who backed them were committed to a change. They knew I was vulnerable and they didn't mind using me as the live issue.

The fight for survival was on, although it was all one-sided. The power was with the liberal majority on the Board of Education.

8

The Reality Of Christ

Forest Home is a Christian retreat center in the San Bernardino Mountains, about one hundred miles east of Los Angeles. Over the years countless thousands have experienced new depths of Christian commitment in this tranquil setting. It is a place of natural beauty with granite canyon walls, clear streams of water rushing around the white boulders and towering pines.

I have only been there once. This was for a Bel Air Presbyterian Church retreat led by Spencer Marsh, pastor of the Brentwood Presbyterian Church. Joan and I arrived at Forest Home on Saturday, the day after Ken Peters notified me that the Board of Education had decided to terminate me as principal of Beverly Hills High School.

I was feeling a deep sense of estrangement and lack of self esteem. This made it difficult for me. I resisted a weekend at Forest Home. I didn't want to be with alot of people. Joan thought it would be a good thing to do, so we went. The theme for the retreat was *Gifts of the Holy Spirit*. It was my first in depth introduction to I Corinthians 12.

Pastor Marsh spoke at the first general session:

> *God gives us at least one gift, he said, Some experience several, and there are many available to us.*

We are to appropriate them, not for self grandeur, but for service and useful purpose as a part of the body of Christ. Our special work is not to be a manifestation of ourselves, but of the Holy Spirit. Our idealism can trick us. We insidiously become our own god for God.

In the name of love we control people and take possession of material things around us. We perceive this as the means to personal value and self esteem, all in the name of concern and caring. We then become disillusioned when the painful waves of loneliness and alienation sweep over us.

Wow! It was frustrating to see how instinctively I put myself at the center when I so much wanted to be God's man. It was treacherous, and I knew it happened because the fruits were so predictable; depression, ineffectiveness and self-depreciation. He was right. He had given me a revelation.

During our Forest Home retreat we shared in small groups. I was with Peggy Cantwell, who headed the adult education program at the Bel Air Church. God used her in Joan's awakening to Christ's purpose in her life so I hold a special love for Peggy.

Peggy asked us to identify what we thought were our special gifts. She referred us to Paul's letter to the Corinthians. I had never known that *administration* could be a divine gift. To my surprise, I found it listed in I Corinthians 12:28, *those with gifts of administration*. I shared my discovery with the group. "I need this spiritual dimension in my job," I told them. I wanted to be more effective in guiding others. I wanted to be more effective in discovering the latent gifts and talents of our staff, and affirming them. My thought processes were alive. I wanted that divine ingredient in my job. I wanted that divine ingredient in my relationship with people.

The Apostle Paul had gone on to say that all the gifts of the Spirit are as nothing, *if I do not have love. I am only a resounding gong or a clanging cymbal* (Corinthians13: 1).

The group prayed for me. It seemed a warm but innocuous exercise at the time. Later I realized this was another important episode on my path to personal growth.

*   *   *   *

It was a late evening communion service on a hill overlooking the lights of the San Fernando Valley. In the informal quiet warmth of a special fellowship within the sanctuary of the Bel Air Presbyterian Church, Pastor Donn Moomaw spoke about the meaning of communion. I had heard the words for fifty years, yet had not really heard them.

This night it was to be different. What happened was to be a major factor in altering my basic approach in meeting with student demonstrators and critical Board members. Donn Moomaw continued with the service. In the low lighting, people went forward and knelt at one of the several round tables at the front of the sanctuary to take communion. I sat and watched. Gradually, I became aware that something new was happening. Intense warmth flooded my body. It all hit me with a flood of emotion that I had never experienced before. I fought to keep from weeping. I did not want to be embarrassed, but it became physically impossible for me to stop the flowing tears. There was no choice now but to just let go. What an unusual experience it was, far beyond my understanding, penetrating my innermost being.

Joan reached over, squeezed my hand, and said nothing. She seemed to understand what was happening. "I couldn't say a word." She later said, "I would have spoiled it for you. It was like you were transported. It was so private, and you just needed me there."

I went to the communion table and prayed. Moomaw put his massive arms around me as I cried. Suddenly, I felt a release. It was a release from the tremendous pressure I had always felt to be totally successful in all that I endeavored to do. This was lifted from me. God was calling me to faithfulness. My eternal future was in His hands.

*   *   *   *

In the days that followed, I continued to rejoice and thank the Christ who had become so real to me. The change in my life was profound. Encountering life within the framework of the Christian gospel, the cross, the resurrection, and all that surrounds the historical Christ event became central in all that I endeavored. The empowering by the Spirit is as valid today as it was for the church in the first century. The experience I had at Bel Air confirmed that for me. Now I believed!

Like other evangelicals I am still overwhelmed by the change that comes from spiritual rebirth. There needs to be a balance. Too often one points to the experience as the yeast, the heart, and the spark for all our endeavors. This results in other committed Christians feeling deprecated because they cannot point to the time and hour they came to the fullness of Christ.

The Apostle Paul never called us to the Damascus Road, he called us to Jesus Christ. His ministry came after many months of trial and growth. It took time for him to assimilate what had actually happened. He had his wilderness experience and time of preparation. To a degree this is what happened to me.

On the other hand, C. S. Lewis, the English critic, poet and author, when asked when he decided for Christ, responded he was not sure. He thought God had decided on him. Although the experiences of Paul and C.S. Lewis were decidedly different, there was a similarity. Both came to their fullness through God's own timing. Both, too, although emotionally different, were undeniably valid. Whether or not one comes in a quiet, growing way which evolves over a long period of time, or in a flash of light on their own roads to their Damascus, there is a birth of the Spirit that transforms human life. But, rebirth is not the end. It is the beginning of a new life with commitment to a divine relationship that carries with it the responsibility for a response forged in study, prayer, submission and mission.

Because this is a story of a crisis in leadership, I share a change in perspective that came as a result of my experience. Leadership is power; but I had not embraced Divine power in the formula. I desired to do God's work in a needy world, a legitimate goal, but my motivation had been virtue. As Richard Halverson, pastor of the Fourth Presbyterian Church of Washington, DC, and later the chaplain of the United States Senate, writes:

The most insidious temptation is not to evil. It is the temptation to virtue. This is the devil's masterpiece, leading people to believe that the way to be God-like is by human effort, that God-likeness is possible by human achievement

I, too, had blocked the power of the Holy Spirit from working through my fallible human hands because I had bound myself in self-centeredness. I thought I was God's man. How could it be? Could I have thought that He needed me more than I needed Him? No one was greater in need of that conversion experience than I.

I have heard both Howard Butt, Director of the Laity Lodge and H.E. Foundations in Texas, and Pastor Donn Moomaw speak on the subject of *Submissive Leadership.* They both used the biblical story of Moses. The message remains with me. Too often they said, we want to achieve more for God. We are not the Moses who killed the Egyptian, but we do try to kill our own Egyptians for God. We do this by embracing human effort to bring about goodness. Like Moses, our intentions are good, but like him we experience a wilderness until responding to a new call to leadership. He had attempted to serve God, and found no reward. Then Moses heard God's call on his life, and although reluctantly out of feelings of inadequacy, he did respond. At a time of weakness and vulnerability, the mighty power of God changed his life. It is the human experience, *For it is God who is at work in you, both to will and to work for His good pleasure* (Philippians 2:13). My awakening continued. It was not to be my work, but God's work in me to do whatever was His pleasure. He wanted me to be what He had created me to be, the human vehicle of the divine life, inhabited by God for God.

All of these experiences brought an awareness that my profession called for new skills in the helping relationship with others. Dramatic changes took place in my approach to administrative leadership because of the way Christ had dealt with me. I no longer resisted empathy for those in pain. A non-possessive warmth, appropriate self-disclosure, and personal vulnerability became tools for understanding and healing.

Dr. Eugene Kennedy, a Catholic Psychologist from Loyola University, Chicago, gave this perspective in a theological study:

> *It is the religious experience of our lives. When someone loves you, when they reveal something of themselves to you, you see more of them. But, something else happens, because by the light of their revelation of themselves you not only see more of them, you can see more of yourself as well. And in this reciprocal process of enlarging each other's life, there is a very real experience of resurrection. It becomes a significant sacramental experience.*

As principal could I appropriate some of these new insights into my relationship with the staff and students at Beverly Hills High School? With Gods help I would try.

9

Steps Forward...

Immediately following my deeper commitment as a Christian, I was released to seek a new relationship with the high school staff. The best way I knew to start was to ask for their evaluation of my performance as principal. I distributed a standard form at a faculty meeting and asked for the evaluations to be returned within a week. About a hundred of the hundred and fifty teachers responded, most anonymously. This proved to be one of the most frustrating, painful and depressing experiences of my life.

Two-thirds of the evaluations were positive. My highest mark was in credibility. There were only two negative responses in this area, but I dwelt on these. Most devastating of all were the evaluations that reported that I came across as cold and uncaring. I rationalized. I was angry. How cowardly to send back an unsigned negative evaluation! After all, my evaluations of the staff had to be made in person and signed in quadruplicate. The teachers were *gutless*! God how could you do this to me? I ventured out in faith, made myself vulnerable, sought a change in my relationship with the staff, and now this.

Pain was instrumental to my needed growth. In prayer I heard again the reply of Jesus:

In the end, for those who trust me, everything

will be all right. Defeat is transitory. Victory is in faithfulness. I will give you no task, no gift, without the power to use it. Your value has been forever established. It is in no way contingent upon or earned through performance. You're filled with the Spirit that fills me. Grow into the self you dream possible. Your value is not established by others but by Me.

It came to me that perhaps I should do something I had never done before; share my feelings with the faculty. This could be risky, but what did I have to lose?

Faculty meetings were held once a month in a large team teaching room on the third floor of the main building next to the bell tower. There was a stage and the desks were tiered from this teaching area. Following the routine reports and presentations, the faculty president turned the meeting over to me.

We have a few minutes until it is four o'clock. I know you are anxious to leave and we will be through by our regular closing time.

We had a good record in holding to our one-hour meetings. This was important to me.

I want to talk with you about the evaluations I received after our last meeting. It's apparent you perceive me in different ways and this is a concern. I take some of the responsibility for the situation because I've never been secure enough to share with you the uncertainty I sometimes have concerning the major problems we face. Sure, we have set up committees to work on school policy and you have been involved, but it has all been rather impersonal; a professional relationship. I need more than that. I guess I need you to know that sometimes I'm not sure I'm right when I make a decision, that I need your understanding and patience when I am wrong. Perhaps this is not what you expect from your principal. If that is the case you are going to be disappointed. But I want you to know me better and I want to know you.

These evaluations show there is confusion concerning me. I have been wrestling with this. You see what I mean about the discrepancies. But regardless, the evaluations are your response; the way you see it and I take them seriously.

What I want to do this year more than anything else is to ask you to help me. Accept me. I'll let down the barriers, when I think it is appropriate, and share with you what is going on. If I seem uncertain and share this with you, accept this not as a weakness in leadership but as a desire on my part to truly be open with you. These are difficult times. I need you. You need me. I guess we just need each other in a way we haven't been free to relate before.

You are all aware that my immediate problem is my pending personnel session with the Board of Education. The majority does not want to renew my contract as principal. I can understand why, even though I see the problem as being much more complex than they do. There are other personal changes going on in my life. These, I feel, are positive but they are effecting my leadership style. This could be confusing. I want to be a more sensitive leader. These days are a struggle for me, but I intend to do the best I can.

This is a hungry community. Beverly Hills, in its own way, is as desolate as another community might be. You know what I mean. You experience it. Everyone is so busy, so success-oriented that there is little emphasis on the deeper relationships so necessary for human development. It is so easy for us to fall into that trap. I don't think I've done a very good job as principal in setting the tone we need. I just want you to know how deeply I feel about this. That is why I am asking for your help.

There was a momentary hush after I finished. Then the faculty broke into an applause that rang with warmth and affection. Several said they had never expected an administrator to express such feelings to teachers. Others I had hardly known sought me out, coming to my office in increasing numbers to let me into their lives.

I shared their pain, their uncertainties and, happily, their personal victories. Most often their feelings were of isolation and loneliness. It seemed to help them, to know I was willing to listen. I learned that the act of listening has a healing quality. What I had feared and resisted for so long, a deep-personal involvement, now became the most rewarding part of my work.

I claimed my gift of administration and with it came fresh and more flexible approaches to a creative leadership style. For the first time I had a feeling I could be an effective part of the solution rather than being continually bogged down in a problem for which there were no answers. This growth in me was coming none too soon. There were still more agonizing student demonstrations ahead and I had not yet faced the Board of Education. It continued to be a time of testing as I fought to retain my old position within a new spiritual framework.

I was finding answers to my need within the context of the Christian life style. My experience as a student in the Extension Program of Fuller Theological Seminary in Pasadena gave me insights and the opportunity for the training I needed. The Fuller School of Psychology in Pasadena, California, under the leadership of Dr. Lloyd Travis, had launched their program where the applied truths of sound psychology and the tenets of the Christian faith became integrated in their teaching approach. This integration, Dr. Travis believed, was the therapeutic agent in the redemption of the human personality. I began to see that within this integrated approach, Christ living out the Divine Word and applying the psychological truths He taught, was the yeast for all human endeavor. I learned more about how we could be ministers of healing, not only in one to one relationships, but also within a group of caring people under the leadership of trained facilitators.

Joan had been asked by Fuller Seminary to start and administer this extension program for lay persons in the Los Angeles area. I enrolled for two years as a student in this program. I learned communicative skills, how to handle conflict in management and, of course took advantage of their excellent classes in Biblical study. Extension students at Fuller were required to be in what they called the *core group*, which was a sharing or support group. Joan and I were among the first students in this program. Later, under the supervision of the Fuller School of Psychology, we were asked to facilitate groups of students preparing for the pastoral ministry. David Bock, a clinical psychologist with the Associated Psychological Services in Pasadena and a Christian teacher, was our supervisor. As lay people we grew through training and experience to be more effective agents for the healing power of God.

Changes continued to take place in my life. I was more and more aware of the impact of my words, my body language, and my responses to people. This intensive small group experience was instructive for the work I was doing in the secular world.

Committing myself to working with student and staff groups in the school district became important and provided a variety of valuable experiences. Some groups were composed of boys, some girls and others were mixed. Time was spent with those identified as *Mentally Gifted Minors,* as well as with others who were serious behavior problems in the school. My efforts could not be easily quantified on a win and loss scale, but growth was apparent and my love for the school and the young people who gave it life continued to grow.

My most valuable resource was a staff group of about twenty people. We became dedicated to one another. Joan and I met with these friends every two weeks at the close of the school day. What loving and caring people they were, representing a large spectrum of responsibility from district administration and supervision, to elementary and high school teaching and counseling. We were men and women, black and white, Christian and Jew, administrator and teacher, all learning to be free as persons ministering to each other and growing in our personal lives.

One good friend, through her tears, confessed, "All my life I knew that I, as a Jew, could never be loved by a Christian. I am in such inner turmoil because I am loved and I just don't know how to deal with this in my own life."

"Everyone at the school, with few exceptions, came to appreciate Robbie as a human being as well as a super administrator," Joan reflects. "This was a big change. It's hard to put into words, but if you saw it in action you'd know there was a softness about him and a gentleness no one but I had seen before."

*　　*　　*　　*

My approach to living out the personal Christian commitment in the secular world is not always clear. How is God's love communicated? I believe in evangelism and in proclaiming the *Good News*, but within me there is deep inner resistance to the belaboring of the gospel with words. To accept my uncertainty and commit this concern to Jesus has, in itself, been an act of surrender.

God, in His creative power, controls our ultimate decision. The timing, if it is to be, will always be His. I began to understand the ways we can live out a Christian life style in the world in which He has placed us. Perhaps this shouldn't always be in the traditional mold, but certainly always in a loving and accepting way, bringing peace and healing to the human spirit. This is a valid ministry.

10

Getting a Heart and a Mind Together

In the midst of legitimate apprehension over my professional status, much of my emotional energy was increasingly directed toward my need for a deeper spiritual understanding. There was a paradox. I was concerned with the uncertainty of my professional future, but I also felt an emerging serenity as I dealt with the spiritual awareness into which I was moving. I also needed to understand intellectually what I had experienced in my heart.

My study in classes at Fuller Seminary encouraged me to examine the theological basis of my faith. As I read the Bible and attended classes and discussions I discovered the book of Romans. Paul began to knock down one idea after another, ideas I had previously accepted as a basic premise for my life. Over and over again the theme of Paul's message came through. We are doomed to failure when we try to gain God's blessing by adhering to a moral code, for no matter how good our intentions are, we will fail to measure up. We will then experience a sense of failure, guilt and growing isolation from God. When the *law* intrudes itself into the process of justification, then *law* multiplies itself and we experience a deeper bondage. This concept attacked the thrust of my life that had put primary emphasis on a moral code and a set of ethical standards. Paul's emphasis is on the fruits of the Holy Spirit: *love, joy, peace, patience, kindness, goodness, fidelity, gentleness and self-control* (Gal. 5:22-23). None of these are in conflict with Biblical law or high moral standards. The concept that my value as a person could never be earned by adherence to the law had troubled me most of my life, but as a result of my experience could now be accepted as a freeing discovery.

Jesus was who He said He was. No longer was He just an ethical standard against which to evaluate a life or just a teacher of teachers. He was the Savior, the Christ. I did not deny the power of the gospel message, the concept of grace and justification through faith. I began a new journey to establish an intellectual base for my Christianity; to understand in my head what had happened in my heart.

> *But now, quite independently of law, God's justice has been brought to light. The Law and the prophets both bear witness to it; it is God's way of righting wrong, effective through faith in Christ for all who have such faith – all, without distinction. For all alike have sinned and are deprived of the divine splendor, and all are justified by God's free grace alone, through his act of liberation in the person of Christ Jesus (Romans 4:21-22).*

For the first time in my life I began to understand. In my commitment to be a good person for God I had been guilty of perhaps the deepest sin of all; taking my life out of God's hands and assuming a personal responsibility for being my own god for God. It was such a subtle but insidious trap. I was no different from

Adam. I had been a humanist, the captain of my ship; and my ship had been sinking. Guilt is a heavy burden and one that at times, I continued to carry. My only answer was to continually encounter Jesus Christ Himself, to keep encountering Him moment by moment in living prayer, meditation, and a deliberate awareness of his presence through faith.

I had identified with Nicodemus when he came to Christ with his question on how to enter the Kingdom of God. Jesus answered:

> *In truth, in very truth, I tell you, unless a man has been born again he cannot see the kingdom of God (John 3:3).*
>
> *Flesh can give birth only to flesh; it is spirit that gives birth to spirit. You ought not be astonished, then, when I tell you that you must be born over again. The wind blows where it wills; you hear the sound of it, but you do not know where it comes from, or where it is going. So with everyone who is born from the spirit (John 3:6-8).*

Blind faith was not enough. I wanted a faith that encompassed my mind as well as my heart. Credibility with myself and with God in this whole business of Jesus Christ was tremendously important. Prophecy, too, brought a new dimension into my thinking. I was impressed with the way Matthew reviewed the credentials of Christ (Matthew One). The Old Testament prophetic establishment of condition after condition for the advent of Messiah and how the birth of Jesus fulfilled these conditions overwhelmed me as being beyond statistical probability.

There are unique paths to Christ, some more emotional than rational, some more rational than emotional. Although I had experienced an emotional breakthrough I sought a theology based on reason, open to criticism and one that was intellectually aggressive. It is human to ponder the basic questions. Philosophy is really nothing more than man's attempt to think things through. I approached the task, not only out of the basic need I have described, but I believe out of the inherent responsibility of every thinking man to establish the truths upon which he can base his life, his conduct and his value system.

I gained a number of insights that led me to deeper understandings and sounder criteria and procedures for determining what I believed. The distinction between *knowing* and *believing* was extremely helpful. This concept came after wrestling with the skepticism of David Hume, the English seventeenth-century philosopher who attacked the foundation of accepted belief, and Immanuel Kant, a German leader of the Enlightenment. During the latter part of the eighteenth century Kant's comprehensive and systematic work in the theory of knowledge brought the Platonist numerical world of *pure reason* and the Aristotelian phenomenal world of *pure fact* together in synthesis. It all made sense. There could be a combining of the pathways to truth. Here was a union that produced a whole or a more encompassing truth. What a breakthrough!

My professors at Fuller Seminary guided me through the journey. I, along with other laymen, came to study after busy days in our professional lives. Dr. Jack

Rogers, in his course, *Thinking Through Your Faith*, dealt specifically with the philosophical problem of reason and experience as it impinges on theology. He terminated a class discussion with several statements I found particularly helpful:

> • *I cannot know that God exists, but I believe He does, because to believe puts my world together and this makes sense.*
> • *Intellectual certainty is idolatry because it excludes the need for faith.*
> • *Believable value is more important than knowable fact.*
> • *Faith is not a rejection of knowledge, but a path to knowledge and then understanding.*

If Blaise Pascal, gifted with one of the finest minds in the history of man, came to the conclusion that the Biblical God can be known, and known only through faith, then certainly I could do the same and not lose my intellectual credibility.

I found an affinity with Soren Kierkegaard, the 19th century religious philosopher who believed life could not be contained within an abstract conceptual system. If one accepts this thesis, then the ground is cleared for an adequate consideration of faith as it relates to Christianity. His view was:

> *The relationship to God is more important than the fact of God. The involvement of our own subjectivity then becomes the truth. I must embrace that which I believe and make it a part of my life to know it.*

It was becoming clearer. How do I know? By incorporating beliefs into a total commitment and experiencing the qualities of the life it produces, sometimes thought of as a foretaste of the divine. The objective of my faith now was not a doctrine. It was a relationship. Here was the answer to life itself. We are here because God wants a fellowship with us. His master plan includes us, in all our limitations, to be His vessels in the establishment of His Kingdom by His indwelling spirit within our human soul.

Paul Tillich, the twentieth century theologian who was a native of Germany before adopting the United States as his country, bound together the realms of religion and culture. In his essay on Faith and Symbols he wrote:

To know God is the ultimate concern, not knowing about Him but participating in Him.

The readings of John Calvin, the French reformer, also helped in establishing my priorities:

Experience the gospel and then the law. Adherence to the Law is the way Christian exhibits thanks to God for grace. It is not the end, only a guideline for Christian living, and the only true path to personal freedom.

What was the Christian theological answer to the question of life itself and why are we here? It was the belief that God seeks a fellowship with us, that He can use us in weakness and in strength to move into His world, meeting the universal human needs for love, personal affirmation, and healing. With this possibility, life takes on the meaning for which we all yearn.

My pilgrimage continued and with it was a renewed sense of mission. Just how real the Christ was in my life would soon be tested as I prepared to meet the demonstrators head-on at the flagpole.

11

Happening At The Flagpole

As the years pass, the exact sequence of events have become hazy, but not their reality or impact. As the decade of the 1960s closed, I was embroiled on several fronts, conflict with the Board of Education, the creation of a new educational program for the 1970's, movement on my own spiritual journey and the dread of facing more student demonstrations. This day would be an apex for those months of tension. Restless student leaders had targeted this particular morning for an all-out demonstration. The Vietnam War was again to be the major issue, although defiance of authority on any level was equally attractive for many.

At about 7:45 a.m. on March 17, 1970, I drove into my parking place in the schools two-tiered parking structure and took the faculty elevator up to the administrative offices. The Principal's office was located on a bridge between the old original building of Beverly Hills High School and the new modern three-story structure that had just been completed to support our new educational program.

As was my practice, I stood by the faculty mailboxes, waiting to say hello to the teachers as they signed in for the day. I had discovered that a brief moment of friendly conversation helped us to know each other better. A middle-aged woman, a native of France who taught in our language department, came running up to me and shoved a mimeographed blue sheet of paper in my face.

"Dr. Robinson! I just picked this up from one of the students!"

"What is it?"

"Look!" she said as she shoved the paper toward me.

It was a notice rather thoughtfully done. It was laid out well and the lettering was neat. It urged the students to walk out of their classes and meet at the flagpole at 10:00 a.m. to demonstrate against the Vietnam War. The teacher, a very strong personality on campus, continued:

"I talked with the boy", she said in a highly emotional pitch, "and he confessed these things are being distributed at various points around campus."

"I see."

"It's calling for a demonstration!"

"Yes."

"Something has to be done about this!"

She didn't give me a chance to respond in a responsible way. She just turned and marched out of the office, breathing heavily as she went and headed for her classroom. I hesitated a few moments before I walked out into the hall. Students were gathered in small groups, buzzing with excitement and pumped for action. I was clearly their adversary, and although some deliberately avoided my look, others openly declared their intention to follow through on the demonstration.

I sensed an overwhelming feeling of power stimulated their determination. I saw in them, no willingness to give or compromise on any issue. The mimeographed leaflets were everywhere. I knew then that within a couple of hours I would be facing another crisis. There would be hundreds of swarming, boisterous and abusive young people, with many others looking on. I was anxious. Mass hysteria is an awesome thing to watch when it takes a destructive turn. I felt so helpless.

As I stood by the office door I tried to show that I was calm and in control. Inwardly, I felt a deep sense of responsibility, but inadequate and uncertain as to how to proceed. Only God could get me through the hours ahead.

A hard-working administrator approached me, the one who had called the police at a previous demonstration. His face was flushed and he was angry as he breathed through his clenched teeth.

"I've found out who's behind this. It's Alan!"

"Alan? Maybe we should talk with him"

"Talk? He should be dismissed! Let's kick him out of school. If we talk, it should only be when his father returns with him"

"I think I'd like to talk with the boy, just to see what's involved."

"I'd dismiss him."

"Have him come to my office right away."

This administrator had been with the school many years. Students who defied the authority of the administration personally offended him.

I was somewhat surprised to discover that Alan was leading this particular demonstration for he had not been one of the main rebel leaders. He had a rather positive, cooperative nature and in the past we had talked easily with each other. He was not an official student leader, but had established a rapport with a fringe element on campus.

Shortly after 8:00 a.m. Alan breezed into my office. I left my desk and sat on a small sofa. Alan sprawled in a chair opposite me. (I had learned that a desk was a physical barrier to communication, as if one were saying, there's a real gulf between us and don't you forget it!)

Alan was about five-foot ten, of medium weight, better dressed than most on campus and sprouted a thin, scraggly beard. I detected likable warmth coming through his arrogant exterior. Alan jerked his head. His light brown hair that had fallen in front of his eyes flipped to the side of his face.

Alan had brought two friends with him who, like their leader, seemed to be enjoying the role they were playing. One boy was small, dark-haired and feisty. The other was heavier, with a black beard and was very quiet. Alan would speak for all three of them.

"Alan, what's the purpose of the demonstration?" I was searching for something other than the obvious.

"It's right there on the memo. It is to protest the Vietnam War," Alan came back.

"Why the demonstration? Aren't there other ways to communicate?"

"Yeah but it's all talk, talk, talk, talk. And talk doesn't mean a thing unless you do something about it." He half-smiled at his friends and waited for their nod of support.

It became clear that this was to be their day. A once apathetic student body was awakening to new feelings of bondage by our institutions. They felt a direct responsibility to speak out against injustice. That was the way they looked at it.

"You know, Alan," I said, "this is creating great

concern for the school. Parents have been calling me. They're afraid someone will get hurt."

"We don't want anyone to get hurt."

"I know you don't, but it still could happen. It's difficult to say what a mob will do. Couldn't we have a meeting in the auditorium for interested students? Let's talk it over before there is another big demonstration at the flagpole."

"Won't work."

"But the demonstration could get out of control."

"No it won't."

"It just seems there could be a more reasonable way to approach it"

"No," Alan shot back, "It's got to be a walk-out. It's got to be. We've talked it over before and have had our demonstrations, but where has it gotten us. This time we'll really get the attention of the community!"

I shifted my weight and probed for a statement that might break through to him. He was so locked in, so adamant, so willing to take chances, and at any cost for the sake of his cause.

"I'm concerned about the Vietnam War," I continued. "There are issues I don't understand. But I'm responsible for this school and I don't want the demonstration to get out of hand."

"That's a risk we're willing to take."

I didn't feel right about threatening him with suspension, as some of my colleagues would urge me to do. That would light the fuse, but I had to do something.

For half an hour we talked, neither one of us moved the other any closer to an agreement. He said they had planned for a loudspeaker to be at the flagpole with representatives from outside colleges invited to speak. Alan knew it was against policy to bring people on campus without clearance, but he wasn't concerned with possible consequences of this action.

"We need outside help to present our position. Kids listen to those college leaders."

"Alan," I snapped, and my frustration began to break through. "I understand your point of view and why you're doing this, but you had better understand my point of view too. When you go out to demonstrate it's going to be my responsibility, not yours. I don't want it to get out of control."

"We have to take that chance! Otherwise we'll never get the attention we want!"

Alan and his friends left the office, moving ahead with their plan with a renewed sense of commitment. I was disturbed during our conversation with the distortion and incompleteness of many of Alan's facts, yet there was honesty in his feeling. When he left there was no direct tension between us, even though we were the leaders of two divergent forces destined to clash later in the morning.

Within the next two hours Alan returned twice to my office. He had agreed to at least keep me informed of any developments, including the names of the speakers coming from UCLA and Cal State Los Angeles. After his last visit he repeated his demand to be left alone to do what he wished at the demonstration.

I received as many phone calls from worried parents and community leaders as time would allow. Most of the faculty had decided on a policy of non-involvement. They would as usual, stay in their classrooms. Two or three did confront me before the demonstration, demanding again that I take strong administrative action against the troublemakers. They wanted a show of force.

I called the Superintendent of Schools, whose office was in the Board of Education building across the street. This was not only proper protocol, but it had become district policy. We called the police and asked them to keep a low profile on the perimeter of the campus. "Keep out of sight," I told them.

I made another phone call to the president of the PTA, who previously had agreed to gather three or four parents to stand on the edge of the campus if another demonstration occurred. Many times actual events had been so distorted by the press or other observers that I wanted an objective group of parents to see through their own eyes how everything was handled. I told them I couldn't stop the demonstration, but would do everything possible to ensure the safety of the students.

Some parents were not able, or refused to understand the dynamics involved. Most were supportive when I explained I merely wanted to diffuse the situation before things got out of control. Any issue arising in the school soon became common knowledge in the *village* of Beverly Hills. There was a grapevine for news I never was able to fully understand. The morning's event was no exception and news of the pending student demonstration rapidly spread through this amazing network.

The clock kept ticking toward ten minutes to ten, the regular time for the morning nutrition. The students would normally be back in class after this twenty-minute break. By that time today the student protest would be in full swing and the outcome was unpredictable.

Lyle Suter had agreed to take still photographs and 16mm film of the action. We had worked through our differences on this issue. A film record would preserve a sense of history and truth regarding whatever would take place. Lyle could see the value of having this record.

At 9:50 a.m. a bell, sounding more hostile and vibrant than usual, signaled the beginning of the nutrition period. Today it was more like a call to battle. I slowly rose from my chair and looked past the secretary's desk and on through a huge plate glass window that enclosed her office.

Immediately I was aware of a strange traffic pattern. Usually the students swarmed up the stairs toward the cafeteria and out to the perimeters of the campus. Today the tide had reversed. This morning the flow steadily and surely, moved toward the front of the school and the flagpole. I resisted a temptation to rush headlong into the throng of gathering students, deciding it would be good psychology to delay until most had arrived for the demonstration.

I walked down the main hall of the administration building to the entry lobby and through the heavy swinging doors to the steps, where I could see the flagpole. Then gradually and deliberately, I attempted to melt into the crowd, watching and being watched, and silently evaluating the circumstances. There were very few faculty members in sight. The teachers, who that morning had so loudly protested the demonstration and who had been calling for such strong action, now played ostrich in their classrooms. I felt alone and conspicuous among 1,500 milling teenagers. They wore what I call pseudo-hippie attire. The blue jeans and T-shirts of the working class look probably cost them a fortune at one of our local boutiques. A pretty girl wearing a long flowing dress kicked off her sandals as an added sign of protest.

The student leaders had already merged at the permanent, black bench that curved in front of the flagpole. One leader was shouting over a portable microphone for the students to assemble. Ninth through twelfth graders were pouring out the gates of the patio area at the southern end of the main building. A crowd with a curious mix of serious and laughing faces sprang up the long steps from the physical education complex on the lower campus. Others hurried from the mathematics wing. Some walked slowly, methodically, from their performing arts and language classes. They were cautious, expectant, and inquisitive.

Others, afraid of becoming personally involved, stared from second-story windows and balconies of an adjacent classroom building. I stood in the crowd, forcing myself to appear relaxed and trying to draw on the source of peace, which I had so recently discovered.

"Hey, Doc, what are you going to do about it?"Dozens of heads turned toward me.

"What's comin' off?"

"This is neat?"

"Hey, what a walk-out, huh? Down with the war!"

"Down with classes!"

And a few of the less serious giggled their pleasure

at temporarily escaping from the academic world.

A newspaper reporter and a television cameraman came on campus. Across the street the director of information for the school district and two assistant superintendents stood at the corner of Moreno Drive near the front of the school. I felt their eyes searching for me.

*   *   *   *

I had made a decision. I had chosen a course of action. If all went well my leadership ability would receive a desperately needed vote of confidence. If I failed, the resulting chaos could lead to my continuing downfall. The last thing I felt like was a victorious Christian. I was more lonely and anxious than secure in the knowledge I was operating under God's will. Strange emotions began to ebb and flow within me.

I was a Robinson. Robinsons are always successful. Robinsons always win. Robinsons fight. Robinsons don't run. Robinsons don't consider their personal feelings, they just look at the cold hard facts and then take responsibility. My great-grandfather had clawed and fought his way to success in California and I would be no exception. This strong hand of the past rested with great determination on my shoulder. But now there was another wise and gentle hand on my other shoulder that was giving me assurance.

You can do it. Live through Me. Act through Me.

*   *   *   *

Alan's knuckles turned white as he clenched the microphone in his hand and stared at the agitated swarm of students facing the flagpole. "This is a time for students to stand up and be a part of the great movement," Alan screamed. "We've got to demonstrate against the injustices of the Vietnam War! The only way we can do this is to let the community know how we feel. This is the time to stand up and be heard!" Alan felt the crowd with him and his energy increased.

"The institutions across the country have given us students a hard time," he continued. "It's important we band together against a government that is corrupt and institutions that are corrupt. If it means marching the streets of L.A. then we'll have to march the streets of L.A."

A Vietnam veteran, sitting straight and tense in his wheel chair, came to the mike. He had previously been arrested for picketing outside an army recruiting station and I recognized him as a former unauthorized speaker on campus. He obviously decided to come right to the point. "This is the time we should take over forcibly!" he began his harangue.

Several college students continued with their speeches, repeating over and over again, "It is time for action; a time to overthrow the government." They offered no specific plan, just that they were to overthrow the government.

This went on for almost a half-hour. Then quite unexpectedly, and at the height of the oratory, Alan looked over to where I was standing. In what I perceived as an almost friendly tone, he pressed his lips against the microphone, and said, "Doc, how about coming up here and giving us a talk?"

I was so surprised I hesitated, neither moving nor

speaking. The students began clapping and yelling, urging me to take the mike. I had always feared speaking before students during times of stress. I had never been booed, but there was a deep apprehension of being rejected, especially when I had sensed their suspicion. Today I felt an acceptance and wanted to respond to their invitation, but was left standing dismayed and speechless. I finally pushed a foot forward and slowly made my way through the clapping students to Alan and the mike. And, amazingly, as I walked a warm inner peace welled up within me. All my years of personal struggle and my pilgrimage for a spiritual meaning in life had been preparing me for this moment. Christ had established my value as a person. I didn't have to prove anything to anyone. All He wanted me to do was to be myself, open, credible and honest. I was freed to share myself with a confused group of students, many of whom were idealistic and seeking a mission and purpose for their own lives. No longer did I have the need to be right. No longer did I need to defend a set of views. I had no need to be the great leader of an outstanding high school. In accepting my weaknesses and recognizing them for what they were, I no longer had to hide behind the facade of strong reactions. In weakness God was freeing me to respond in Christ-like strength. I was experiencing the biblical message. *God choses to do His work through fallible human hands.* I sensed his healing power.

Dear Jesus, the words escaped as a whisper from my lips, *make this a special day. Somehow, show how to transmit the new love I feel in a way that will be helpful and real. I can't do it without You, and I call on your Holy Spirit.*

I took the speaker's stand, relaxed and free. I reflected on all I had heard, not the profane words, not the angry statements, and not the exaggerated demands. Rather I responded to their pathos, to their longing, to their confusion, to their distrust, and to their questioning.

Stillness hung in the crowd. They had wanted to be heard, and somehow I verified they had been heard. It was then, with as much openness as I knew how, I shared my own idealism, my dreams, my disappointments, my confusion and my frustrations. I spoke of my need for them and of our need for one another. I confessed:

> *I have often made difficult decisions, not really certain I was right, but out of the expectations of the leadership responsibility I hold. I want to be a servant-leader, giving you the very best educational experience that I can.*
>
> *I've been listening to you, and I think I hear your deep frustration with our times, especially with what's going on in Vietnam. You're distressed with your leadership and the institutions of our country. You're frustrated because you don't know how to effectively deal with all of this.*
>
> *Even though I would like to see you use other ways to express your concerns, I feel a little more sympathetic to what you are doing than I might have been in times past. I was in school when this country was at war. Everyone supported it then because we had been attacked at Pearl Harbor. I fought for our country then because I knew it was the right thing to do. I*

didn't begin to face the moral decisions you must make. Today things are so different. It is a very uncertain time for you, and I am sorry.

They were quiet. They were paying attention. They were listening.

In the past, as your principal, I've wondered if I have overreacted in dealing with many of you. Sometimes I really haven't heard what you've said because of my own confusion. If you are frustrated, imagine how I feel. So often you have challenged me while I have been wondering how to adjust and still meet my responsibility to the school.

I treasure being your principal, but many times I wonder if I exercise the kind of leadership this community expects of me. I share the frustration and the concerns you're experiencing. It's time we really understood one another. We need to work together rather than to fight.

I represent the establishment and rules and regulations because that's the role I've chosen. It's expected of me. Yet it's a difficult time for leadership. I wanted you to understand that in a different way I, too, have some of the frustrations you are experiencing. It's time we came together as a school and as a student body. I appreciate the fact Alan invited me up here. We've been together many times this morning, and he knows my concerns about handling mass demonstrations and of what might happen. I was afraid of this situation because things can get out of control.

> *I hope we can go back to class and sometime later continue this dialogue with one another. But, as I said, it's really out of my hands. I can't control the situation. I can't make you go back to class.*
>
> *As far as I'm concerned you may stand out here and talk until noon. I'll be here with you. You've walked out of class, I know how you feel, I sense your frustration and your indignation at what's happening in our country. I hope you feel you have been heard. Maybe in the weeks ahead we can build and move ahead in a more positive way, working with one another. When you're ready to go back to class, then go.*

The crowd was unusually quiet and meditative. A couple of the previous agitators from UCLA had fled the campus after they were through speaking, but several still mingled in the outskirts of the demonstration, waiting for the next move.

Alan was the one who took the next step. Taking the microphone gently from my hand, he began;

"It's been great to be out here. I'm glad we could talk and have this opportunity to protest. I'd like to thank Dr. Robinson for coming out. The demonstration is over."

As I left the flagpole my heart was warm because I realized that what had just happened was the reality of the Holy Spirit being involved in the human process. I hadn't struggled as I spoke. It was low-key but incredible as far as the kids were concerned or they wouldn't have reacted in the way they did. A soothing blanket had been thrown over the crowd. The tension had dissipated. A crisis was past and a relationship between the students and an institution had gone through a healing. New avenues of communication were opened and never again would I be faced with a student walkout at Beverly Hills High School.

*   *   *   *

The flagpole incident remains with me as a significant time of growth and understanding in what it means to live out a more effective Christian life style in the reality of our secular world. The demonstration also served as a springboard for increased personal contact with the students.

As I was learning, there was a theological foundation upon which my new leadership approach was based. Some of these understandings had come almost instinctively as an integral part of my spiritual birth. But some of my understandings came through my continued study.

Howard Butt, of the H.E. Butt Foundation, Kerrville, Texas, senses the true call that emerges from the Watergate judgment. He writes:

> *It is time for a new vision. What does it mean to be a leader who walks in the light of openness? What does it mean to be a leader who sees himself first as Christ's servant?*
>
> *The story of Watergate is not primarily about subterfuge, dishonesty and manipulation. It is the profile of man and what happens in his use of raw power. It is the story of every man, of you and me. We have ignored Christ's good news about leadership.*

Because of my experience the Beatitude, *Blessed are the meek for they shall inherit the earth*, takes on new meaning. No longer do I think of a meek person as one drained of all courage. I see the meek as those who accept their human limitations and inadequacies and are willing to stand before God and accept His help, His power and His blessing.

Strength comes in the dynamics of this relationship between man and God. There is power in the willingness to let the will of God override a particular position or the means of operation we have chosen. It's a paradox: in weakness there is power, in power there is weakness.

Henri Nouwen, former Professor at Yale University and the premier communicator of a relational theology, in his book, Reaching Out, gives a perspective on what is involved in the helping relationship:

> *Administrators who can be freed from their inner need, out of insecurity, to control and impress are then truly freed to receive the actual messages students are carrying within them.*
>
> *So often inner truths are buried beneath anger and frustration, and neither the sender nor the receiver is free to perceive the true nature of the longing within the human heart. Sensitive leadership seeks to free those served by hearing the message and, in this receptivity, create the climate for the healing where individual gifts in each one can more nearly be identified and nurtured.*

Father Nouwen captured the Gospel message in that discourse. Christ does come to free us of ourselves so we can exercise our unique gifts under the unction of the Holy Spirit and then, and only then, become free to know the wholeness God in His love has ordained.

*   *   *   *

All of us who have sought the leadership role are imbued with the need to be decisive and strong in the administration of our responsibilities. It stems from that insatiable drive to be in control. Our entire cultural background suggests that strength comes from the exercise of power in the sense of being able to dominate and control rather than in releasing the energies of others. In other words, be tough, throw your weight around, stand against the wind and don't be pushed.

I suggest my growth has encompassed an acceptance of sensitivity, of expressed feelings and of openness in the leadership role. I seek a freer and more creative approach as I work through my administrative responsibilities. The strong reaction in a given situation can be tenderness, sensitivity, an inclination to judge less, or perhaps even inaction. I don't want to limit God. I seek the freedom to let Him work through me with a voice filled with the force of the storm or with the listening ear of a tender and understanding spirit. Life is made up of its victories and defeats, its moments of elation and despair. One who has seriously committed his life to Jesus will live life in the totality of its pathos. I'm convinced, when one accepts the fact that ultimate worth is established in faithfulness to Christ, not in the win and loss record, God frees that person to be used in His strength in ways which are often exciting and miraculous.

These truths of the Gospel message, as demonstrated in the *Happening at the Flagpole* continued to jump from the pages of the Bible into my own life as the spring of 1970 pushed dramatically toward summer.

12

No Longer A Stranger And Alone

Howard Butt in his latest book, *Renewing American's Soul*, begins his chaper on *Estrangements* with this quote from rock icon Jim Morrison of The Doors, who captured not only the mood of the sixties but also the perennial human condition when he wrote the lyric,

> *People are strange when you're a stranger,*
> *Faces look ugly when you're alone.*

*   *   *   *

The following weeks on campus were very different than any I had experienced before in the twenty-five years I had spent as a teacher and administrator.

Beverly Hills High School had gone through the stress of releasing all dress and grooming codes on campus. The students responded by coming in outlandish dirty and unkempt attire. We were not a pretty student body. I felt the pressure unleased from a disturbed and concerned community over the general demeanor of the students.

It was difficult not to be repulsed by many that took on the appearance of the *hippie-drug culture*. I had communicated, in subtle ways, my feelings of contempt for many of these young people who frequented the majestic halls of the school.

After my conversion experience, my feelings about these students changed drastically. I began to see them more as I believed God saw them. I felt a compassion and a love for people I never before thought possible. They must have felt the change that was taking place in me, for many that rarely spoke to anyone outside of their immediate peer group became more open and responsive. We began to communicate with one another in very personal ways. One on one encounters of significance happened frequently and in the most unexpected and exciting ways. A new plan was in operation. Of that I was certain. Coincidence could not account for the people who were coming into my life and who were letting me into their lives at a depth I had not known before. I was free of the fear of being rejected, that fear that in the past had closed me off from many of the young people on the campus.

*   *   *   *

There was a teacher of *communications* at Beverly who was a very creative young man. I first met him in New York where I went on occasion as a member of the College Entrance Examination Board. I recruited him to teach in the special program that I had envisioned for our expanding curriculum. He was a maverick in his own way, and many of the *alternative* students, as I defined them, responded to his teaching. Some of these students told him that they would like to talk with me. He was open to the idea that, maybe, I had changed enough to deal with something like this. When he invited me, I went. It was a weird situation. How did I get trapped into this?

I was ushered into a back storage room where the kids were sitting on a mattress. Their spokesman invited me to sit down with them. (Me on a mattress! The idea of a principal of a great high school sitting down with a bunch of *hippies* on a mattress was ludicrous.) I sat down. The young people went on with their discussion about the high school almost as if I were not there. They were not leaders in the student body. I perceived them to be almost a sub-culture to the majority of our students. It soon became apparent that as a group they had not *checked-out* on our society, as many in that time did. They were showing thoughtful concern and searching for answers. Gradually they brought me into their conversation. I discovered that beneath their alternative demeanor they were very bright and sensitive people. I became very real with them and they accepted me. Good relationships developed and I did find out many things about the school I had not known and this gave me an important access into the way young people were thinking. In some strange way I was being loved and accepted, freed from some of the generalized judgements many of us were making. That, I am sure, made me a better principal.

> *Happy is the age in which the great listen to the small., for in such a generation the small will listen to the great.*
> –The Talmud

*   *   *   *

There were many interesting encounters with

parents. A principal's job entails meeting one crisis after another, and I was usually successful in defusing many potentially dangerous and explosive situations.

I was aware that my approach in relating to parents modified somewhat after experiencing God's forgiveness in my life. I no longer felt driven to always make my decisions on just the basis of arbitrary policy. It was easier for me to listen and I became less judmental and more compassionate.

Beverly Hills High School had a well defined, excellent program designed for students identified as mentally gifted. We had labored long with district committees to develop the program and set up the board polices under which it was to be administered. Honor and Advanced Placement classes were well established and the universities accepted the excellence of our program.

Formulas used for admitting students into these classes were comprehensive and adhered to by our academic departments with sometimes undue tenacity. I was reluctant to make exceptions to policy, even though now within my personal philosophy I felt comfortable in seeing policy as a guideline for decision making.

Many on the staff were interpreting any compromise as a weakness in administration. Also, my official evaluations to the Board of Education indicated that I had a tendency to operate outside of strict policy. This was true and I felt pressure from this criticism. For me there was a fine line between assuming authority and submitting to authority in the area of policy decision making when it involved an individual life.

Four eight-year elementary and middle schools in Beverly Hills graduated students into the high school. Parents, in many cases, held unrealistic goals for their children. The majority of the student body was Jewish and culturally they were imbued with a deep need for educational achievement. This proved to be a strength as well as a weakness in working with the young people. Those who could succeed intellectually were stimulated for continued competition and advancement. They were the *winners*, but some of these so called *winners* became losers in life because they surrendered to pride, arrogance, independence, thoughlessness and an inclination to hurt others by their insensitivity.

There were others who often, because of limited academic ability or emotional or psychological problems, rebelled. This rebellion was expressed in various ways. Some resorted to overt behavior and became serious disciplinary problems. Others retreated into themselves, attended classes in a physical sense, but were passive resisters doing just enough work to pass, or in some cases they deliberately failed. Motivating this segment of the student body persisted as a major problem.

* * * *

One day a particularly aggressive father barged into the office. He had a son who was in the eighth grade at one of the intermediate schools, and the high school counselor, as directed, had programmed the boy into the classes he would be taking as a freshmen in September. The father's request that his son be enrolled in an honors biology section had been denied because the student had fallen slightly below the arbitrary level set on a standardized test for admission to the class.

He had requested a conference with the Principal, so I had a good idea that a problem was coming. I was prepared. The Counselor and the Science Department Chairman were with me when the father came to the office with fire and anger. I shall never forget the scene. Here was that little bald headed man, with a bantam rooster strut about him, puffing himself up to be assertive. I recognized him immediately. He was a Beverly Hills resident with large property holdings in the Los Angeles area, married to a large woman who was a well-known character actress in Hollywood. I knew instinctively what had happened. Here was, in spite of all his wealth, an insecure little man who had been sent by an aggressive wife to give us an ultimatum.

This he did! "Put my boy in honors biology! I've contributed substantially to the board members' campaigns and I can get anything I want. Don't waste my time. Just give me a *yes* or a *no* right now so I can go higher if I have to!"

He went on to explain that money can influence any decision, and that he had the money. Further, his boy was going to Harvard and he was prepared to endow Harvard with the amount necessary for admittance. His boy was to be given a program that would qualify him for any school in the country.

This of course hit me as an extremely wild and irresponsible claim. Ordinarily, I would have been repulsed by the manner in which he had presented his demand. My human reaction was to meet his anger with anger, or more accurately, just stubbornly stand firm on the policy as established.

This didn't happen. Somehow (it still amazes me), I felt compassion. I felt the love and concern of a father for his son. I just knew the fear that gripped him, a fear that success for his boy was going to be blocked by an institution he perceived as cold and uncaring. I listened. . .

Then, with sincerity and understanding I spoke. "Your action on behalf of your son, is the most poignant statement of love for a boy from his father I have ever heard. I can relate to what you say, for I love my boy, too." He melted before us.

For me, that was a gift from the Holy Spirit. My job was to love and to listen. Then somehow in God's own creative way the solution would come. My new friend now responded in a soft and emotional way. At first the Department Chairman and the Counselor looked shocked. They were dismayed. The most amazing thing to me about the whole episode was that I never had to say another word. The Department Chairman took over. "I think we can work something out," he said. . . and they did.

The fact that we decided the boy was capable of a chance to enroll in honors biology, that we broke established policy, that later the student earned one of the highest grades in the class and that he graduated from the high school with honors is important. But more important is the miracle of divine love and what it can mean in human relationships.

It is important to add I was not always successful in my human encounters, and I found it increasingly difficult to accept and live with feelings of alienation. I was vulnerable and open in ways I had not previously experienced. Yet my days were filled with rich and unexpected gifts. These were the gifts of other human lives, shared and trusting. I no longer felt alone.

* * * *

I remember walking through the patio area one morning on the third level of the new classroom building. A door was open to one of the English classrooms and I caught a glimpse of a boy seated at a desk. He was the only one in the room.

Ordinarily, I would have passed, engrossed in thoughts of the total responsibility for the school. This morning I entered the room and sat down beside a boy I did not know, but I did recognize him as one who had some behavioral problems in school.

He was a marginal citizen, one who often had to be challenged as to why he was not in class. This morning I stopped with no intention of confronting him. He seemed to immediately sense this and we began to talk. He was an attractive blond well-groomed boy who would have preferred to wear his hair longer. That was out of the question for him, because he came from a Navy family where that was not tolerated.

"I saw you sitting here," I began. "What's going on?"

He began to cry uncontrollably. I was with a boy who was in deep personal pain. I just put my arm around him as he struggled through a wave of emotion and waited until he was ready to speak.

"I'm really in bad shape," he choked. "My dad and

brother were killed three days ago in an airplane crash in Alaska." He sobbed again, but eventually went on with his story. "My mother and father are. . .were divorced. We had a lot of fighting going on in our house and I think I was to blame. They didn't like what I was doing and argued a lot about that. Finally, my dad just took off with my little brother for Alaska. I'm responsible. . .they got killed."

He buried his face into his arm, soon gained some control, and then lifted his reddened eyes to me. "I don't know what to do? How can I go on living, knowing that I. . .I." He couldn't finish.

I pressed his arm in a gesture of sympathy. "No one can really understand the load you're carrying, how you feel so alone. You think you can't talk it through with your mom. Your dad and brother are gone. You're distraught and confused and alone because no one will understand. That's a lonely place to be isn't it?" He couldn't answer because he was still crying, but he did nod his head and leaned over so I could hold him.

A relationship was established between us. It came because, at a critical time in this boy's life, through God's love for me, I was free in a new way to move into another's life. God had brought me to a troubled boy for whom He, too, grieved. I sensed God had worked through my fallible hands with an effectiveness I had not before experienced. These occasions of personal encounter were frequent, emotional, exciting, and often painful as well, as I entered more deeply into human suffering.

*   *   *   *

I turned in a crowded hall to a girl who was standing surrounded, but alone. "Can I help you?" I asked. Her eyes moistened and I knew that even in a noisy corridor, crammed with pushing bodies, God was at work to alleviate voids of loneliness and despair when there was sensitivity to His call. Here was a girl I would not necessarily have picked out in a crowd, even though her groomed sandy reddish hair and plain dress gave her attractiveness. Perhaps it had been her sad and searching face that had attracted me.

"My whole life has blown up," she said. "I can't go to college."

"Do you need to talk?" I asked. "Would you feel free to talk with me?"

She looked amazed. "Yeah, I guess so."

"It's really crowded in the hall and I have a few moments. If you care to come to the office we can talk."

We sat on the couch. She told me that there had been a big blow-up at her home the previous night. Her father had walked out on her mother, taking with him the only hope she had for the financial help she would need to enter college. Her mother, having to readjust financially, wouldn't be able to send her to the university. At least that was her perception of the situation and she was crushed.

"Maybe I can help you." I called a Rotary Club friend who was the general manager of the prestigious J.W. Robinson department store on Wilshire Boulevard.

"John, I have a young lady who needs work."

I had looked up her record and found she was a good student and a responsible person. I felt strongly that I should help her and explained that if she could get a job after school she could start earning money during this last semester in high school and then perhaps work full time during the summer.

"Send her over," was John's positive response. She was employed in a good position and in the fall was enrolled at UCLA. Her continued education was important, but I relate the story because of the divine quality I see in the incident.

*   *   *   *

For years I had been wrapped snugly in a cocoon of stiff-jawed determination. To a degree absolute codes had governed all situations life had thrown at me. The problem was, as protected as I felt in that cocoon, it had cut out a lot of light from my life. It wasn't until through God's grace, I had with his help, emerged into a growing, relating Christian. It was not until then that I realized what I had been missing. Through God's power I had been able to spread my wings, bask in the *light*, and fly. . . *no longer a stranger and alone.*

13

Nailing Down The Board

As the board meeting, which would determine if I would get a contract for another year approached, Joan could see an increasing strain affecting me.

The Sunday before the meeting we met after church with a very good friend and colleague and his wife. He was assistant superintendent of the school district. We were counting on him for support, but as he prepared to leave his mood seemed to shift.

"Robbie, I hate to say this, but I really feel you don't have a chance. Probably your best bet is to just bow out gracefully." They were gone before we had a chance to reply.

Joan and I sat in our study, silent, and stunned. These friends, ones who wanted to be supportive, saw only futility in our struggle. I sat quietly, drained and depleted. It felt as if my world had ended.

"Robbie," Joan began, "I don't believe him. I don't believe him for one minute. He's wrong. You know he's all-wrong! I know you. I know what you believe in and what you stand for. I know you love that high school and you're doing a superlative job. If they lose you they'll lose what they need. You have a responsibility to do something about it!"

"There's nothing I can do."

"Yes, there is. We'll go to the church and we'll talk

with someone there and get some counseling."

"But that's for people who have problems."

"We have problems."

Joan called Deanne Hendricks, our good friend and assistant pastor, and told him we needed to talk. He said to come right over.

We spent a long time talking with Deanne, explaining the circumstances of the impending board meeting and all of the background information. Deanne waited patiently until we finished.

"I agree with Joan," Deanne said. "The others are wrong and you know I don't believe in beating your head against a stone wall if there's nothing to be gained. But there's a principle involved with not only your life, but also the lives of your students. You really believe in what you're doing. Everything is constructive and you're right in the middle of your work. You're not finished yet. There's a time to stand and a time to go. You have to make that decision. If you want to stand up and tell the board what you have to say, then go ahead. I believe you should, and I'll pray for you."

"I was beginning to think I was kind of crazy," I answered. "Everyone was saying I was wrong except Joan."

"I don't think so," Deanne said. "You know I really care about this. I believe in what you are doing. I also know that as senior pastor, Donn Moomaw would be the most imposing person you could have with you. You tell me you would be allowed to have someone with you at the hearing. He is the one who should be sitting beside you in that meeting with the Board. They know him, not only as your pastor, but also as an effective member of the State Board of

Education. That will carry a lot of weight, believe me."

I had wanted support. Spiritual support, of course, but primarily I knew I needed someone with political weight standing with me, and Donn certainly had that requirement. He was openly excited when I explained the situation and asked if he would join me at the meeting.

Under the rules, an employee called into a personnel session with the Board is entitled to two representatives at the hearing. Donn, would be one. By this time I was encouraged to be more aggressive in my own behalf. I decided to ask Hugh Depatori, our school librarian, to also attend the personnel session with us. Believe me, he was far from being the school librarian you might picture. He was equally as tall as Donn, over 6'2" and about 220 pounds, a dark good-looking Italian. Not only was he the high school librarian, he also was a member of the Secondary Education Council and more important, he was president of the Beverly Hills Teachers Association.

"Hugh," I said, "Would you consider being with me when I go before the Board for my personnel session?"

"Great! You know I believe in you and what you stand for."

This response gave me a tremendous boost. The backing of the teachers' organization, which he said he would bring with him, would provide added leverage for me.

Other events miraculously began to fall in place. Dr. John French, the president of the Beverly Hills Administrative Organization, took the initiative in getting our organization to file an official letter to the Superintendent and the Board for my support.

Dick Keelor, the football coach, had taken off on his own. "Hell," he said, "You can't wait around for that Board to do the right thing. Pressure! That's all they understand. I'm tired of teachers standing around with their hands out. You're right and I'm going after them!"

Peters called me into his office.

"You tell Coach Keelor to cool it," he said. "He is getting way out of line and it's your responsibility to stop him!"

"You don't tell Keelor anything he doesn't want to hear. You know that," I replied. Peters didn't pursue it further. I knew he admired the coach, not only because he had built an excellent athletic program, but because he knew Dick wouldn't be pushed around.

Keelor had the officers of his parent's athletic booster club putting pressure on individual board members in my behalf. This was a questionable practice to say the least, but greatly effective in politically astute Beverly Hills, where the candidates raised large sums of money to run for these offices. In any discussion of effective styles of leadership, you cannot dismiss the model of Dr. Richard Keelor. I needed a Keelor, but the school also needed me, if any permanent healing was to continue to take place.

The afternoon of the personnel session with the Board arrived. Donn Moomaw came to the high school and was ushered into my office. I brought him up-to-date on the situation. When I finished, he said, "Let's pray."

This was a new experience for me at Beverly Hills

High since my own petitions had always been hurried and silent, not vocal and deliberate. Joan was with us, supporting me all the way, as always. Donn says she's the president of my fan club. Our prayer was the kind where you really knew you had made contact. We trusted the situation into the loving care and keeping of God, who knew more about my future than we did.

"We believed God would work miraculously for a miracle in the encounter," Donn recalls, "It might not be the miracle of Robbie remaining as principal, but the miracle of having a calm, peaceful self-assurance. I was committed to the fact that even though the circumstances might not change, Robbie could change to fit the circumstances, no matter what they were," Donn said. "I was more concerned about Robbie's ability to cope with a crisis than I was with the crisis itself. To prepare him for the crisis was a bigger goal to me than to pray for a specific victory in this encounter."

Joan waited alone in my office, while Donn and I walked across Moreno Drive to attend the four o'clock meeting. Hugh Depatori was waiting for us. When I was called into the boardroom these two hulks of men were on either side of me. This, and the fact that I felt well prepared, gave me confidence. There was a new assurance of authority within me and I felt quietly under control.

When a board member asked me a question I would answer it head on, not in a challenging way, but with appropriate initiative. It was a strange kind of meeting because it was not difficult. It didn't last too long. Neither Donn nor Hugh said anything, because the president of the board just acknowledged their presence and thanked them for coming.

After their initial questioning of me, a heated argument began between the two factions on the board. One young lawyer, who represented the minority, became aggressively supportive of me. It was apparent that the majority of members were beginning to feel the pressure. They asked for my solution. That was a twist.

"I would like at least another year to bring the MOD 70 curriculum into fruition," I said. I felt I needed at least another year to bring this innovative program to completion. "You can have my resignation as of July 1, 1971."

My request was granted, and the session was over. This bizarre decision would soon explode to become the political issue in the Beverly Hills Board of Education election. But for now, at least, I had a reprieve. I was flabbergasted at the dispatch with which all this had proceeded. We left the board offices and returned across the street to the school. Kully and Joan were waiting on the steps, that late afternoon. "How did it turn out?" he asked anxiously.

"I've got another year, Kully."

"Good."

He put his arms around me and Joan did too.

*   *   *   *

The next, battle centered on the board elections. I was in the very eye of a political hurricane. The day of voting came to Beverly Hills and, for the first time in history, an incumbent board was defeated. One member was not up for re-election. The person taking his place supported me. A pro-Robinson candidate defeated one anti-Robinson member. This, together with the re-election of another supporter, drastically changed the complexion of the board.

Suddenly, I found myself in a position of leadership that could not have been earned in any other way than under a test of fire. The new Board tore up my resignation and gave me a new contract. I was the undisputed principal of Beverly Hills High School, this year, and next year and to retirement. Or so I thought.

14

From The End To The Beginning

During the early 1970's there was a big change. Now with the support of the Board of Education and the backing of the community, I was secure in my job. I could stay as the Principal of Beverly Hills High School until retirement at age sixty-five. The school was going smoothly. It was like a whole different place, and I was relaxed and comfortable in my role.

After the Board of Education election many on the staff who had avoided me when my job was in question returned. Almost everyone wants to be associated with a winner. When one is perceived as a loser only the truly loyal come forth. This had been a painful lesson to learn.

What about the school superintendent? Kenny Peters and I had a positive, professional relationship in the early years of our association. But, gradually, because of some mixture of our egos, pride, and perhaps some stubbornness on my part, the walls of our defenses were kept up. I attributed this resistance to what I perceived as his undue authoritativeness. Regardless, this would lead to confrontation. After my new leadership status had been established, I began to emerge from under his firm grip. As he began to come on stronger with his directives, a tension developed between us. It was a problem we would have to face.

For the first time Peters began giving the Board negative evaluations when he rated my performance. I had never received anything but positive ratings when I had administered in a less relational leadership style. He felt I was beginning to run an independent operation at the high school and that communication was poor between the school staff and the central office. "You had better join the district," he said, with a sarcasm I began to hear more often.

Secretly, I knew that communication was poor, too. But, I felt it was poor because we hadn't developed a climate where the staff could be honest and open. Unless we could demonstrate a trust at the leadership level, we couldn't ask teachers and students to relate to one another in a positive way. I knew this was true, but I hadn't spoken to Ken Peters. I just swallowed my feelings, and tried to let it pass. I let it pass because I didn't know how to confront him with my perspective. I was afraid. I knew how others on the administrative staff felt because they had come to me with their concerns, but I needed to protect them.

I shared all of this with Joan and she responded. "You take a paternal attitude toward the sub-administrators. You think you can protect them by acting as their spokesman, and yet you are not even doing that. You need to lead them, and let everyone talk it out."

"I know how they feel," I shot back in frustration. "They don't want to complain, except to me." That ended the conversation.

The next day, I went to Ken Peters and requested that the top district administrators meet with the leaders of the high school staff.

"We want to talk about this problem of poor

communication between us. Hopefully, through talking with one another we can bring some clarity to the concerns we all express. I don't think we can make any progress until we do this." I tried not to show the nervousness I felt.

"I'll decide," Peters said.

I sensed he wanted me to know that he was in control, and I left his office apprehensive that I had taken on more than I could handle.

Soon I received a memorandum setting the time for the meeting that would take place. I prayed a lot about this. I wanted to be as constructive as I could. It had been difficult for me to invite this kind of confrontation and I was apprehensive that the meeting would not go well. All nine administrators finally met around a big walnut executive table in a conference at the district office.

"I have raised some questions about the effectiveness of the high school administration," Peters began. "There is a lack of communication between the district and the high school. Dr. Robinson feels part of the responsibility is at the district level and has asked for this meeting. I'll give the floor over to Dr. Robinson so he can state his piece."

Right then the gauntlet had been thrown down. There was no retreat for me now. Mr. Peters expected a response.

I know the district is task oriented and I'm task oriented, too. We have a tremendous responsibility to see that the school runs smoothly. Teachers need an environment where they can teach, and the students need to continue to have an excellent educational experience. That hasn't always been easy to accomplish in these difficult times. Yet, I feel the task would go better if we could become more relational in our approach to that task. We need to take time to relate to the teachers and the students. It has not been an easy period in our history. We can't be effective leaders if we can't model those caring qualities in our own lives. There isn't a single person here who doesn't know what I am talking about.

For years I have seen us sit around this very table, playing our little games. I know I have been afraid to speak out in any honest way in fear of being put down or punished. There is a better way to relate to one another. Communication has broken down, but that's because we don't feel a part of a team. You don't build loyalty through directives. I take some responsibility for this, because I have been silent, even though I have resented some of the memorandums we have gotten. I have perceived that they were sarcastic or caustic. I know I have been less than cooperative when this has happened. This is not good. We have a job to do, as Ken says, we're task oriented. But I know our objectives would be better reached if in working through our goals, our people felt more openly involved. We talk about an administrative team, but for me it has been largely words. I don't know how well I'm saying it, but you know what I mean.

It was time for me to stop and let someone else speak.

"I want to make one thing clear right now," Peters

grumbled. He stood up and the red flush on his face signaled trouble. "I'm task oriented! I always have been task oriented! I always will be task oriented! You can have your relational approach, but by God! Do your job!"

His fist came down hard on the table. "We're not here to run a popularity contest."

"I'm task oriented too," I countered, frustrated that he didn't begin to understand the dynamics of which I was talking. "But the task would go better if we could model our own relationships in being open and vulnerable with one another. I'm tired of playing games."

Peters asked some of the other administrators to talk and it became very tense for about two hours. As we stumbled and fought to a close, Peters announced, "This is the most frustrating experience I've ever had in my life." He turned abruptly and walked out.

From the first, the other administrators had responded to what I had tried to do. Even though it was a very painful experience, I felt good I had attempted what I had. It was clear how I felt, and my colleagues responded on an individual basis in a very supportive way. They agreed we needed to stop just acting out a role with one another. We needed to relate in a more positive way than we had in the past.

This incident helped to establish my leadership position in the district. I'm not saying this to run down the superintendent, because I'm very sympathetic with his position and his frustration. There are many restraints on the top administrator in the district. Some are political and very real, but some, I think he inadvertently put on himself because he was ultra-conscious of the role he thought he had to play. I understood this, because I had been there. One positive result of the confrontation was that never again did *poor communication* between the high school and the district staff come up as an issue.

* * * *

Psychologically I had accepted that God intended Beverly Hills High School to be my place of ministry in this world and accepted my work as a manifestation of the divine purpose for my life. I was inwardly content with the idea of my professional career being established until my mandatory retirement.

Then, one day during the summer of 1975 the phone rang in our Tarzana home, not an unusual event. This call, however, would spark a dramatic change, which would uproot our lives. Our friend, Bill Cody, the director of Laity Lodge in the Texas Hill Country was on the line.

"Howard Butt asked me to call you," he said. "Would you consider coming to Texas to head a new project for H. E. Butt and Laity Lodge Foundations? We are looking for a director of lay theological education. You'd work with us and a dozen theological schools in the Southwest."

Howard Butt! I was well acquainted with his dynamic Lay Ministry and the support his successful family grocery chain had given to Christian Leadership Conferences across the United States. It was a challenging thought but I dismissed it as less than a responsible thing to do. I was at the height of my professional career and holding the position of principal at the high school was still personally rewarding.

Joan was well established at the Fuller Theological Seminary as the administrator of their extension program and Dana, our youngest daughter, was in the midst of a happy and successful junior year at Beverly Hills High. Our two oldest children were married. Gail's husband Steve was completing a second residency, this time in cardiology, after serving two years as a Navy doctor. They had recently moved to nearby Long Beach. Our granddaughter Noelle was a great joy to us.

Our son, Tri, and his wife, Nancy, were on the ranch in the northwestern corner of Los Angeles County. He taught school in Antelope Valley. Their little daughter, Kate, was a fifth generation Robinson living on the original property my parents and grandparents had developed. Our heritage in southern California had great depth and we delighted in being with our children.

"I'm not looking for a job," I said. "Thank you, but the last thought in my mind is to move to Texas."

"Think about it, anyway," Bill Cody responded. "I'll call you back in two days."

After I hung up the phone, Joan confronted me.

"I heard three things in that conversation which really bother me. If we're going to share things with each other, and if we're a partnership, then, number one, you didn't ask me anything about it. You didn't say, Joan and I will talk about it. Number two, you said Dana was going to be a junior in high school. If you're going to use Dana as an excuse, you should ask her. She may have her own ideas about this! Third, we haven't prayed about it!"

"Well, you're right." And so we talked. "Would you really consider living in Texas?"

"I didn't say that," she shot back. "All I'm saying is that we should be open. We're all in this together. You don't know, this might be a whole new ministry opportunity for us. At least we should talk with Howard."

It was true, I didn't fully understand what Howard Butt had in mind or just why he had called me.

"How do you think Dana would feel if by some chance we did decide to move?"

"Ask her."

"O.K."

Later I asked Dana how she would feel about a possible move. She surprised me.

"I've never lived in a small town. This would be my only opportunity to do that. I'm so lucky to be here. Since I was born so late in your lives, what you do shouldn't be controlled by me. You need to do what is best for you and I will adjust. I'll be off to college in a couple of years anyway."

She wasn't quite sixteen years old. Then Joan joined in. "You need to consider that in a couple of years you will be at maximum as far as your retirement benefits are concerned. You're not ready to retire. I know you. You will always need a challenge and a cause. I think we should at least go to Kerrville and meet with Howard Butt."

That made sense to me. It was the responsible thing for us to do, and we did need time to pray.

Bill Cody called back two days later. He was the

spokesman for Howard Butt. I was prepared to give him an answer.

"We'll come to Texas to talk with you and Howard. That's all I can say. But if we do come, there is something you will need to consider. I can't come just for another job. If we come it will have to be on the basis of a joint ministry that includes Joan. Howard Butt might have a problem with this, so let me know."

I felt strongly about Joan's involvement. She had more experience in building educational programs for the laity than I did, and it would be unfair to tear her away from her leadership position in the Fuller Seminary Extension Program without further capitalizing on her talents.

Arrangements were made and Joan and I boarded a Continental Airlines flight to Texas, landed in San Antonio and drove west for sixty miles over Interstate 10. The rolling hill country slipped by as we moved easily over the green ridges covered with cedar and Spanish oak, past the valleys of the Guadalupe River and through the limestone bluffs and aquifers laid down in some prehistoric sea.

It was shortly after the noon hour when we dropped over the last ridge and entered Kerrville, Texas, home of the H.E. Butt Foundation. What a picturesque and peaceful setting it was, two identical English stone cottages shaded by large pecans, a giant oak and a magnificent Magnolia tree. Howard Butt was waiting for us in his spacious, paneled office, furnished tastefully with antique furniture and comfortable couches.

"So glad you could come," he greeted us, and we

met his wife, Barbara Dan, and the rest of the staff.

For the better part of the next two days, we talked. Naturally, we needed clarification on the organization of the foundations and the specific expectations of our proposed work.

"We have three foundations," Howard explained, "the H.E. Butt Foundation, the Laity Lodge Foundation and Christian Men Inc. Your work would be within the Laity Lodge and Christian Men Foundations. Both are designed to bring quality educational programs to the *Laity*. You would be responsible for some retreat work at Laity Lodge, sixty miles west of here on two thousand acres along the Frio River. But, primarily you would be developing a new program, a joint project between our foundation and twelve seminaries in the Southwest. We are anxious to bring the resources of the seminaries to areas throughout the country and provide a program of continuing education for the *Laity*."

Howard Butt had a vision for the laity to which we could respond. "We have generated an age of specialization and professionalism," he explained, "and advertently or inadvertently abdicated our spiritual role in the world to a professional clergy not always prepared to minister in the earthy relationships of the market place. Lay ministry is naturally ecumenical. We don't work in Baptist labor unions. Those in public education don't teach in Methodist institutes nor do we live on Catholic streets or buy in Presbyterian stores."

Howard was getting wound up by this time. Joan and I loved his enthusiasm, his intensity. He continued.

"The ecumenical nature of the lay ministry is not always accepted by the established church hierarchy.

The conflict you have gone through in the secular world is nothing compared to what you will experience as you begin to work with mature and professional Christians."

"You mean the battle over the Bible?"

"No, that can be a front. I see it more as an attempt to protect the status quo by both the lay and professional leadership, to hold tight to their power in the Christian world."

This sounded familiar.

"You make it sound pretty formidable."

"You could make a contribution as the director of this program with the seminaries. You know administration and you could build creative educational models for us. I know that. You would not be a threat, either, as you worked with these mature and professional Christian people."

"Thank you. Joan and I see our work as both equipping and healing. Men and women committed to living out their lives under the unction and power of God, whether professional church workers or lay persons, we need one another. We are all an important part of the body of Christ."

Howard continued, "That's right, but we need a renewal in our institutions and that comes only when Christ moves into individual lives. Then the family is renewed, and then renewal of our institutions can become a possibility. For the Christian, all of one's work should be Holy. That's renewal. That's my vision. That is what we are all about."

Joan was actively involved in the discussion, and it became apparent to the staff what a valued added dimension she would bring to the ministry. We could share the job and work together.

At some point it became clear that we needed to respond to this call. Aspects of the mission were frightening to me. There was so much ambiguity. We would be starting from scratch, but this was a challenge, and God had prepared both Joan and me for this dynamic in leadership training.

*   *   *   *

The problem of determining God's will in a given situation has always been difficult for me. I have resolved it the best I can by putting the decision to a test:

- *<u>Does it make sense</u>? God expects us to take responsibility for our lives.*
- *<u>Is there an inner witness of the Holy Spirit</u>? Through prayer the Spirit can bring clarity and peace.*
- *<u>Have I sought the counsel of my family and trusted others</u>? All fellow Christians are human and fallible, but their counsel can be helpful if there is discernment.*
- *<u>Do I have an excitement and a sense of desire</u>? When our will is enmeshed in God's will, there usually comes an inner joy and freedom of spirit.*

When these factors are in synthesis, it seems time to move out in faith. But, it is only in retrospect that I see confirmation that I have moved within the will of God. That was how it was in this decision that would drastically change our lives.

15

We Say Goodby...

Leaving the position as principal of Beverly Hills High School was more difficult emotionally than I had imagined. I was not running away from a difficult relationship. I wanted to go. But, I still was not prepared for the loss, the pain of severed relationships and the grief that flooded in. How do you say goodbye? I would walk through it step by step.

I needed to talk with Ken Peters first. He was not in his office on the day Joan and I flew back from Texas. "You might reach him at his home," his secretary responded. "He is going on vacation tomorrow." She sensed the importance of my request.

I called Ken. "Could I see you this afternoon? I would like to talk with you before you leave on vacation."

"Yes," he answered. "Come on over to the house."

I left the school on that August afternoon in 1975, drove west on Wilshire Boulevard through the canyon of rising condominiums that mark the entrance to Westwood, and then swung north toward the San Fernando Valley. As I drove over Sepulveda Pass, the western reaches of the San Fernando valley were free of the smog that often pollutes the area and blocks the magnificent view of the far mountain ranges of Los Angeles County. I could look north to where Interstate 5 bisects the first range of hills and then on for sixty miles.

There on the far horizon, stretching along like a giant whale's back, cutting the surface of the sea, was the 6,000-foot ridge of Mt. Liebre. I saw the dark shadow of Coldwater Canyon on the south escarpment of the mountain where as a young boy I had the encounter with the lion. There in that wilderness, so close and yet so far from Los Angeles, I had ridden with the cowboys, rounding up the wild cattle in the early days. There I had hunted and killed my first buck. Over the far ridge was my old family ranch, my grandchild living there now, the fifth generation, on the same piece of property. There still were my roots, my place; as Paul Tournier says, *A Place for You*. Every rock, every tree just as it had been for fifty years, and now I would be leaving. It was so final and my talk now with Ken Peters in a few minutes would make it official. Then there could be no turning back.

I drove through the interchange at the bottom of the grade, then west on the Ventura Freeway to the Reseda off-ramp, and south again into the foothills where Ken Peters lived in his Tarzana home.

"Come in," he said when I arrived. "The family is out. Let's sit in the living room." His manner was relaxed and cordial.

"Thank you." I got right to the point. "I did need to talk with you, Ken. I've been going through a time of re-evaluation," I began, "and an opportunity has opened up for me. After a lot of thought I've decided to resign as principal of the high school and join a family foundation in Texas. I wanted to talk with you first."

There was a long pause . . . Then he took a heavy breath. "When do you want to leave?" he asked.

"I would like to finish out the year. January 1st is the date I have in mind."

"This is going to create a problem. I wish I had some alternatives at this point," he said. "Your leaving will create a void. I just hate to see it happen. We have gone through some hard times." He seemed to be thinking back over our years together. "You have done a good job," and then he looked right at me. "I don't want you to leave with any strain between us. Thank you for coming out here to talk." Within all the friction that had been between us, there was also an unexpressed warmth and mutual admiration. I sensed both of us wanted to break through, but we didn't.

"I appreciate your letting me know," he continued, "because at least now we can get the board to approve the process we will need to get under way to select the next principal."

We didn't pursue the *tension* or *strain* concern to which he had alluded. That was the way it was. But now I accepted that under his professional competence and persona there was a tenderness I had not seen. He was a good man.

There was finality in our meeting, an inability to retract a cutting loose from an identity I could never regain. I was empty inside. In a way I had not known before, I would live out the balance of my life in faith. I had expected a faith commitment would bring with it an invigoration and excitement. My predominant feelings were of pain and apprehension . . . All through the long Autumn of 1975, I don't think Joan or I once questioned the rightness of our decision, not even as she sobbed in an empty house as our personal belongings rolled off in a van bound for Texas, or in the quiet of a late December afternoon when I said my last goodbye to those with whom I had been closest and shut my office door for the last time.

*   *   *   *

Lyle and Kully had come separately for a personal goodbye. "I have something for you," Lyle said. "They aren't much, but I wanted you to have them." He tried to be offhand.

"I can't believe this, Lyle. What a talent! They are so life-like. And to think you did this for me." He had proudly opened a portfolio with a series of portrait sketches depicting my life from the time I was a year old until I reached professional life. It was a labor of love and they now hang in our home. We both knew it was more than a gift. It was symbolic of our warm relationship that had been forged and tempered in the emotional fire of social change. We had been dramatically involved.

*   *   *   *

Kully had been unusually quiet. We both sensed that my leaving would create a void in our lives that would never be replaced. But the time had come when Kully and I knew we had to face the reality of our separation. He had come to say goodbye.

"I think you're the best friend I've ever had, Kully. We have had something very special between us and I'm going to miss you." I had difficulty putting into words the love I was feeling for this man.

"It just will never be the same, Robbie," he responded. "I know that. The talks, the sharing. How many times in a man's life does one have this kind of relationship? I'm going to be lonely around here without you."

We never did say goodbye. We just embraced. Then he turned and left me in an empty office.

*   *   *   *

I was burying a rich past to breathe life into a future I could not fully understand.

The people of Beverly Hills were good to us. Night after night there were farewell occasions. The warmth and affirmation from these special friends blessed us.

My official retirement was held in the school cafeteria on the third floor, just off the beautiful landscaped area in the heart of the new building. The local civic and school committee planning the retirement decided it would be more appropriate to hold the event in the school rather than in one of the elaborate hotels in the community.

My night of retirement, long dreaded as an exercise of traditional protocol, turned out to be a very special time of needed finality. It wasn't necessarily the many dignitaries who were being generous in their remarks. It wasn't the beautiful resolutions presented from local, state and federal governmental bodies. It wasn't the music, and the humor. More important, it was the warm feelings I felt from the people I loved. These friends, who didn't understand my motives for leaving, nevertheless, still supported me with their love and caring.

Adele Nadel, twice the president of the PTA and a confidant during many of my crises, set the initial tone for the evening:

Two years ago, I heard of a love-in. I didn't know exactly what that meant then, but I certainly know what it means now. Tonight this is what I would call a real love-in, people together with love in their hearts for Robbie and Joan, special persons who have touched our lives in such a unique way.

The pain I felt in saying farewell seemed congruent with the flow of my life as it moved toward a destiny I could accept only on faith. I was experiencing a death and with it the crucifixion of a personal power. The conflict between my human desire to hang on to an identity as it had been forged out in the competitive world and my vision of an identity based on faithfulness to the sovereignty of Christ no longer was an intellectual exercise. To a degree that I still did not rationally understand, I was submitting. My friends were cutting me loose with love and support.

The speeches were made, the final tributes given and I was invited to respond. After some light banter and my expressions of gratitude, I closed with a thought which I had developed as part of our school's yearbook theme on Rainbows.

As I write on this December day, I am hit personally with the poignancy and timing of this theme. There's a deep symbolism in the rainbow. It marks an interval between the old and the new – a bridge between past and future, storm and a new beginning.

This is where I find myself as I say farewell to a school and the people I have grown to love. Now I step forward into another life filled with challenge and hope.

I find myself in the rainbow because it was created by God as a covenant of His love for each of us.

The story is told in Genesis as God spoke to Noah and established the covenant that there would never again be a flood to destroy the earth. To affirm this promise He set the rainbow in the cloud as a symbol of the agreement between Him and the earth.

When I cloud the sky over the earth, the bow shall be seen in the cloud. Then I shall remember My covenant (Gen. 9:14-15).

A covenant of love commands a response, and for me that response appears to be another career in the lay ministry, this time in Texas. I take much of Beverly Hills with me, lessons in how to create effective educational models, new dimensions of human understanding, administrative skills in tapping the unique gifts of others and the joys of human involvement.

All of these understandings you have helped me learn. They will be invaluable in my work ahead. The bridge between the old and new is very real for me, a bridge of color, hope and warm memories of my past seventeen years as principal of a great American high school.

Thank you for the unique opportunity I have had and the rich experiences I have lived. We are very much a part of one another and for this I am happy. For this I give thanks. Goodbye, and may God bless and keep you.

*   *   *   *

Three weeks later we were on Interstate Highway

10, driving east between the Rio Grande and Pecos Rivers in route to our new home in Kerrville, Texas. The early morning sky began to lighten. It was cold. Wisps of snow blew in traces across the highway as we drove over the mountain pass to Van Horn.

"I can't believe we are doing this," Joan said. "It seems like a dream. This is all unreal."

I knew, too, she was thinking about our sixteen-year-old daughter who was half-asleep on the back seat. Dana had not stood in the way of our decision and that had solidified her as a member of the family team on this adventure.

In a few moments Joan broke the silence again. "I brought a tape of the sermon Howard Childers preached at Bel Air. Do you remember it? *The Day the Wind Hit the Sails*. We need to hear it again." She slipped the tape into the panel below the dashboard.

Howard had been the Associate Pastor at the Bel Air Presbyterian Church in the hills above Los Angeles. He is a talented and relational Texas A&M graduate who organized the small group ministry in our church. In a moment his familiar and warm Texas drawl came alive again as we sped along.

> *This morning I'm going to talk with you about Pentecost. That was the day that the wind hit the sails and it changed the world. This never would have happened if those inadequate, frightened and confused people, in the doldrums of their lives, had not in obedience and faithfulness hoisted their listless sails. God filled their sails, and they moved out in a new power under the unction of the Spirit to bring healing to a waiting world.*

Joan reached over and I felt her hand on my arm.... Then the gray Texas sky eased into a sunrise of gold, and with the new day came again *the assurance of what we hope for and certain of what we do not see (Hebrews 11:1).*

Epilogue

A quarter of a century has passed since the *Happening at the Flagpole*. Joan and I celebrated our fifty-fifth wedding anniversary this year. We have built four homes and lived in three states since leaving Beverly Hills High School. Unexpected opportunity for continued ministry has been the impetus for these changes.

On our 50th wedding anniversary we were high in the air over the vast reaches of the Pacific. These were the same skies that fifty years before I was flying on quite a different mission. Now we were on our way to New Zealand to teach in the South Pacific School of Missions where we would be working with young people seeking direction for their lives.

All of these years Joan and I have been blessed with continued opportunity to be with wonderful people seeking relationship as they pursued their spiritual journey. Today we are living in Boise, Idaho where our son Tri Robinson pastors a dynamic church. Not a week has passed in all these ensuing years that Joan and I have not been involved in the teaching and sharing of the *Biblical Truth*.

*   *   *   *

"Why don't you finish your manuscript?" Joan encouraged. "You do have a story to tell."

"It is on my heart," I answered. "I just wonder if it's current anymore?"

"Your experience is more current today than ever.

The lessons you learned have a timeless application," Joan insisted. "The seeds sown by the counter culture during the tumultuous times of the 1960's have now changed America. Leaders are questioning. Everyone is questioning. You tell your story!"

*   *   *   *

How does one determine validity in leadership? In a world that measures validity in terms of results and secured power, this is not an easy question. As some of the scales have dropped from my eyes, I seek a leadership somewhat different from the world's. I want to be a leader who does not depreciate others, but values, enriches and frees those with whom I work. I want to be a leader who exudes love and concern, recognizing that we are all trapped in the Human condition. I want to be one who responds to God's gift of Grace, for me the eternal hope for mankind and the restoration of our institutions.

Effective leadership calls for a vision that is dynamically communicated and has a strategy for accomplishment. There is an added quality present in the Christ model of leading. It identifies the latent God-given gifts and talents of those with whom one works. It affirms the divinity of the Spirit as detected in the human personality. It seeks to nurture and help others in their maturing process. It is a leadership that lifts people rather than one that is repressive and controlling. This is *Servant Leadership!*

By the continual metamorphosis of being conformed day after day through the indwelling of God's spirit, the secular can move toward the Holy and our institutions can become more of God's kingdom. In theological terms this is called *the process of sanctification*. The idealism of this position should not dissuade us. Our Lord calls us not to assured success in the eyes of the world, but to obedience and faithfulness to His eternal plan for our life.

House of Representatives

TRIBUTE TO DR. F. WILLARD ROBINSON

HON. THOMAS M. REES
OF CALIFORNIA
IN THE HOUSE OF REPRESENTATIVES
Tuesday, December 2, 1975

Mr. REES. Mr. Speaker, I am proud today to call to the attention of my colleagues in Congress the name and the achievements of Dr. F. Willard Robinson.

Dr. Robinson is a man who has devoted his life to the service of others, particularly the youth of our Nation.

His early years were spent in his own education, at Long Beach Polytechnic High School and at the University of Southern California. He achieved high scholastic honors and also distinguished himself on the debating team and on the track and cross-country teams.

As was the case with so many others, Willard Robinson's education was interrupted by World War II. He defended his country as a pilot in a carrier-based torpedo squadron, operating in the Pacific area. He served 54 months active duty as lieutenant in naval aviation.

After the war, Willard Robinson returned to the University of Southern California for graduate work in education, to better equip himself for the teaching of young people. He earned the M.S. and Ed. D. degrees in education as well as secondary and general administrative credentials.

Dr. Robinson has contributed to the educational process and the educational systems of the State of California and the United States in many ways. He has worked without respite in the California and National Associations of Secondary School Administrators. He was also a Director of the College Entrance Examination Board.

Since 1959, Dr. Robinson has concentrated most of his efforts at Beverly Hills High School where he has directed and supervised the development of an educational program without equal. He has provided the kind of leadership that has resulted in the steady improvement and broadening of programs to meet the needs of the students through the most difficult period in the history of education in our country.

The strength of a man is permanently etched against the background of his accomplishments. This man's courage has borne him through military fire and pioneer flight to the forefront of education. Nurtured in the heritage of stern religious forebears, a man displays his power to grow as he bends with the times. To change from strict traditionalism to open, people-oriented leadership is a measure of a man's sensitivity and involvement with the future. Climaxing a life with a third career routed in idealism and dedicated to building models for today's youth is the pinnacle of achievement. Willard Robinson is such a man, a unique human being of talent and integrity.

I ask the House of Representatives to join me in saluting an outstanding American, F. Willard Robinson.